Greetings *from* St. Augustine

Donald Spencer

209. HOMEWARD BOUND ON THE DIXIE HIGHWAY, FLORIDA.

DRIVING BEACHES.
...ine, Florida

503'

400'

503

Colorful Flamingos at Casper's
Ostrich and Alligator Farm
St. Augustine, Fla.

Schiffer Publishing Ltd®

4880 Lower Valley Road   Atglen, Pennsylvania   19310

Other Schiffer Books by Donald D. Spencer:
Greetings from Daytona Beach
Greetings from Ormond Beach

Designed by Mark David Bowyer
Type set in Architecture / Korinna BT

ISBN: 978-0-7643-2802-2
Printed in China

Published by Schiffer Publishing Ltd.
4880 Lower Valley Road
Atglen, PA 19310
Phone: (610) 593-1777; Fax: (610) 593-2002
E-mail: Info@schifferbooks.com

For the largest selection of fine reference books on this and related subjects, please visit our web site at **www.schifferbooks.com**
We are always looking for people to write books on new and related subjects. If you have an idea for a book please contact us at the above address.

This book may be purchased from the publisher.
Include $3.95 for shipping.
Please try your bookstore first.
You may write for a free catalog.

In Europe, Schiffer books are distributed by
Bushwood Books
6 Marksbury Ave.
Kew Gardens
Surrey TW9 4JF England
Phone: 44 (0) 20 8392-8585; Fax: 44 (0) 20 8392-9876
E-mail: info@bushwoodbooks.co.uk
Website: www.bushwoodbooks.co.uk
Free postage in the U.K., Europe; air mail at cost.

Contents

M-2—"Pudgy," the Porpoise, at Marine Studios, Marineland, Fla.

M-8—Mother and Baby Porpoise at Marine Studios, Marineland, Florida

Chapter One
Introduction

St. Augustine is the oldest permanently occupied European settlement in the continental United States. It was founded in 1565 after other settlements in Florida failed, mostly because of hostile natives or hostile weather. Despite wars between European nations or with Native Americans, St. Augustine, with its 144 blocks of historic buildings on the National Register of Historic Places, survives to preserve layer after layer of history and as testament of how this nation was won, developed, and lives on.

'Old World' atmosphere abounds everywhere like a London fog. Numerous narrow streets flanked by crumbling walls, gardens, and venerable buildings with overhanging balconies provide all the necessary ingredients for a bona fide Old Spanish city. The City of St. Augustine has done a marvelous job of historical restoration and has permanently depicted and preserved, in stone, clay and coquina, five centuries of history, from the time of the early Timucua Indians down through the successive periods of Spanish, English and American occupation.

Apart from being the oldest city in America, St. Augustine may also be one of the most widely photographed communities in the country. The city's best known monument, the Castillo de San Marcos, along with its rustic City Gateway and narrow streets, have long been favorite targets for photographers and picture postcard publishers. But old photographs and postcards are also perishable resources. For this reason they have been reproduced in this book to preserve some of St. Augustine's picture postcard heritage. Most of the scenes in this postcard collection date from the early 1900s through the mid 1950s and is a fascinating way of studying the history of St. Augustine.

Greetings from St. Augustine, the oldest city in America. Circa 1940s, $3-5.

The monetary values of the cards shown in this book are provided as a guideline for collectors. The values are based upon the rarity of the postcard scenes. Condition has not been factored in and should be considered when evaluating individual postcards. The postcards used in this book are from the collection of the author.

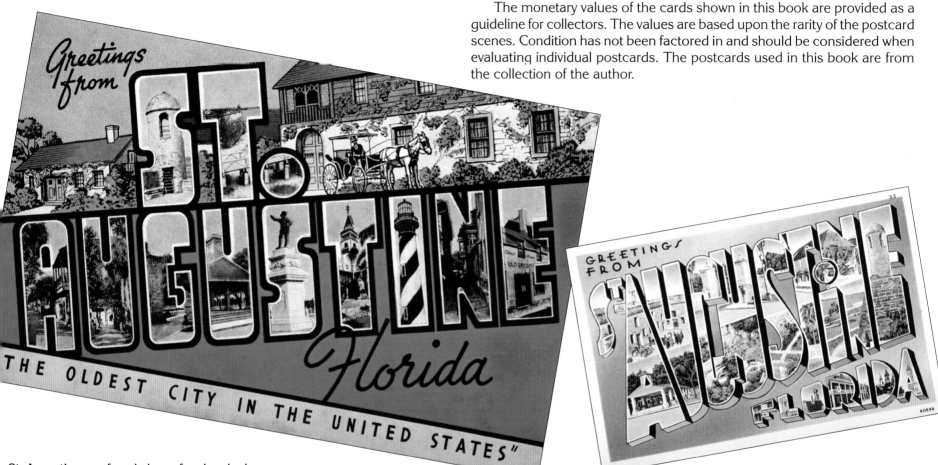

St. Augustine was founded over four hundred years ago by the Spanish to protect their treasure fleets traveling from the New World to Spain. Circa 1940s, $3-5.

St. Augustine is located on the Atlantic Ocean between Jacksonville and Daytona Beach. Circa 1930s, $2-4.

A Religious Beginning. Religion was a driving force in establishing and maintaining this far corner of the Spanish Empire. Circa 1930s, $2-4.

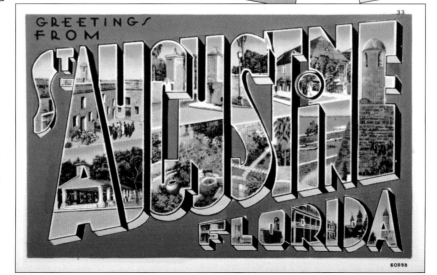

Greetings from St. Augustine. A view of the city from the Castillo de San Marcos. Circa 1990s, $1-2.

Florida Map. This 'Greetings from Florida' postcard shows the location of St. Augustine and other major Florida cities. Circa 1914, $3-5.

Chapter Two

A Brief Historical Overview

A New World Unfolds: 1513-1565

• In 1513 Juan Ponce de Leon, in search of gold, sailed from Puerto Rico, and on March 27 he landed slightly north of St. Augustine. Ponce de Leon named it Florida, having discovered it on Easter Sunday. The Spaniards planted a cross, unfurled the royal banner and took the oath of allegiance to Ferdinand, in whose name they took possession. Thus Florida was added to Spain's growing and far-reaching New World domain.

• In 1521 Ponce de Leon attempts unsuccessfully to settle Florida.

• In 1562 Frenchman Jean Ribault explores the mouth of St. Johns River.

• In 1564 French explorer Rene de Laudonniere arrived in Florida in the neighborhood of St. Augustine, but kept on sailing north to St. Johns River. Here, where Jean Ribault had previously erected a marker bearing France's arms to indicate possession, Laudonniere established Fort Caroline, thereby challenging Spain's title to Florida.

Ponce de Leon Statue. Located in St. Augustine, this bronze statue is a replica of the original that, since the early 1800s, has stood in the plaza of San Juan de Puerto Rico, near the cathedral where the explorer is buried. Circa 1950s, $3-5.

The discoverer of Florida was Juan Ponce de Leon, a former governor of Puerto Rico. Ponce de Leon sighted the eastern coast of Florida on Easter Sunday, March 27, 1513, while on a trip in search of gold and silver. Ponce claimed the land for Spain and named it Florida. Circa 1930s, $3-5.

S. A. 113—Ponce de Leon Monument and Circle, St. Augustine, Fla.

Statue of Juan Ponce de L
in Fountain of Youth Par
St. Augustine, Florida

Ponce de Leon Monument and Circle. This magnificent statue of Ponce de Leon holds a commanding position overlooking beautiful, silvery-blue Matanzas Bay in the nation's oldest city. The figure of Ponce de Leon is cast from old cannon. Cancelled 1951, $3-5.

Statue of Juan Ponce De Leon. This statue of Juan Ponce de Leon is located in the Fountain of Youth Park in St. Augustine. Circa 1940s, $3-5.

First Spanish Period: 1565-1763

• In 1565 Pedro Menendez de Aviles, one of Spain's most eminent of men, was sent to Florida to head an expedition comprised of thirty-four vessels and 2,600 people, to colonize the country and suppress a Huguenot settlement near the mouth of St. Johns River. He landed at St. Augustine on August 28, establishing his colony, and then marched to exterminate the Huguenots, which he accomplished with great vigor and cruelty. Menendez is credited with establishing the first permanent settlement in the United States.

• In 1580 Pedro Menendez Marquez discovered Coquina on Anastasia Island.

• In 1582 Spain consolidated her dominance over Florida with the conversion of Indians to Christianity. As a result, missions reached into the most populace of aboriginal habitation north and west of St. Augustine.

Menendez Coffin. The headboard and coffin of Pedro Menendez, the founder of St. Augustine. Circa 1940s, $1-3.

FOUNDING OF ST. AUGUSTINE, FLORIDA BY SPANISH UNDER MENENDEZ IN 1565

The Founding of St. Augustine. On September 8, 1565 with banners flying, trumpets sounding, artillery booming and 600 voyagers cheering, Spanish explorer Pedro Menendez de Aviles, set foot on the shores of St. Augustine. In honor of the Saint whose feast day it was when Menendez first sighted shore, he named the town St. Augustine. In quick order Menendez and his men made friends with the Timucua Indians, moved into the "great house" of their village, built a moated fortification, and mounted four brass cannons. Circa 1950s, $4-6.

9

• In 1586 the famous English filibuster, Sir Francis Drake, arrived at St. Augustine with twenty-one vessels and destroyed both the wood log fort and the town. The principal public buildings of St. Augustine at that time were a courthouse, a church, and a monastery. After the departure of Drake, the Spaniards rebuilt the town.

• In 1647 three hundred families totaling 1,500 inhabitants occupied St. Augustine.

• In 1665 a party of English buccaneers, commanded by Captain John Davis, made a descent upon St. Augustine with seven small vessels, and pillaged the town.

• In 1668 an English pirate, Robert Searles, surprised St. Augustine, looted it of everything of value, and left sixty of its people dead in the streets. This evidence of St. Augustine's weakness finally caused Spanish officials to act. It was the attacks of Sir Francis Drake and Robert Searles that prompted the construction of a stone fortress.

• In 1669 Queen Regent Marianna of Spain signed an order authorizing the building of an impregnable stone fortress at St. Augustine. Instead of wood, the new fort was to be built of coquina, a shell-rock formation found in abundance on Anastasia Island across the bay.

• In 1670 the English settlement of Charleston, South Carolina posed a threat to St. Augustine.

Moon over St. Augustine. A nighttime view of the Matanzas River, the Bridge of Lions and downtown St. Augustine. The Bridge of Lions, with its 23 pairs of arches, bascules and four tile-roofed towers, connects Anastasia Island with St. Augustine. The bridge is a centerpiece of St. Augustine's character. Circa 1940s, $2-4.

St. Augustine, the nation's oldest permanent city, is one of the most important historical areas in America. It is located on the Atlantic Ocean between Jacksonville and Daytona Beach. Circa 1993, $1-2.

- In 1672 work on St. Augustine's new fortress began and occupied the better part of the next twenty-four years. The Spaniards named it Castillo de San Marcos or Castle of St. Mark.
- In 1683 French and English pirates captured the Matanzas Inlet watch tower, but are defeated near the Castillo de San Marcos.
- In 1686 Spain attacks or drives back French pirates that landed at Matanzas Inlet.
- In 1691 a sea wall was built to protect the St. Augustine shoreline from sea erosion.
- In 1695 Jonathan Dickerson, the shipwrecked Philadelphia Quaker, traveled to St. Augustine. He found the fort, curtain, and bastion walls thirty feet high.
- In 1702 the English destroy the Indian missions while enroute to attack St. Augustine.

- In 1702 the English colonists under Governor Moore laid siege to the fort, and for three months the garrison and citizens were confined within its walls. Though the English occupied the town, they soon found that there was little chance of taking the fort. They eventually set fire to the town, destroyed practically all of the buildings, and withdrew.
- In 1703 the citizens of St. Augustine started rebuilding the town using coquina rather than wood for many of their dwellings.
- In 1704 a series of English and Indian raids destroyed a chain of Spanish missions in northern Florida.
- In 1727 Colonel Palmer, of South Carolina, with a force of three hundred men, tried, but could not force an entrance past the gate of St. Augustine.
- In 1733 the settlement of Georgia brought English enemies closer to St. Augustine.

Aerial view of Castillo de San Marcos, the oldest fort in the United States. An attack by the English in 1670 solidified Spanish resolve to better fortify St. Augustine. Groundbreaking for the fort took place in 1672, with the basic structure completed by 1696. Constructed of massive blocks of coquina stone quarried nearby, the fort was built by Cuban engineers including Ignacio Daza. Skilled stone masons from Havana, slaves and Indians participated in its construction. With its twelve-foot thick walls, encircling moat, dependable water supply and latrine flushed by tidal action, the entire 1,500 residents of St. Augustine found refuge here in times of trouble. The coquina structure measures 324 feet by 311 feet. There are twenty-nine casemates and two other rooms within the Castillo. Castillo cannons commanded the harbor entrance. Circa 1969, $2-4.

• In 1737 new cannons and other fortifications were added to the Castillo de San Marcos.

• In 1738 the Spanish governor of Florida granted freedom to runaway British slaves and established a free black settlement, Fort Mose, about two miles north of St. Augustine.

• In 1740 General Oglethorpe of Georgia advanced south with a strong force and attacked St. Augustine both by land and sea. After twenty-seven days of ineffectively bombarding the fort, Oglethorpe lifted the siege and returned to Georgia.

Cannons. This imposing fort, built between 1672 and 1696, has dominated the St. Augustine townscape for over three hundred years. The star-shaped fortress withstood all sieges imposed by troops in the 17th and 18th centuries. This photo was taken around 1890. Circa 1990s, $1-2.

• In 1741-42 engineer Ruiz built Fort Matanzas at the inlet to control inland waterway leading to St. Augustine.

• In 1742 the Spaniards from St. Augustine marched against Georgia, but were forced to retreat.

Fort Matanzas. If an enemy ship slipped through the Matanzas Inlet and sneaked up the Matanzas River, it could attack St. Augustine from the southern flank. Wooden watchtowers warned against such attack until the completion of Fort Matanzas in 1742. Circa 1990s, $1-3.

• In 1743 Oglethorpe made a sudden descent upon Florida and marched to the gate of St. Augustine when his Indian allies captured and slayed forty Spaniards under the very walls of the fort.

• In 1744 St. Augustine had proved its worth to Spain and was rewarded with more liberal aid. It was now a picturesque Spanish colonial town of 3,000 souls.

• In 1763 a treaty established peace between Spain and England and Florida was ceded to the English in exchange for Cuba, which had been taken by an English fleet during the war.

The British Period: 1763-1783

• In 1763 the devastating news announced in March shocked St. Augustine citizens far more than if enemy fire had suddenly exploded from across the harbor; Spain had ceded Florida to England in exchange for occupied Havana and other territorial possessions of value to Spain. Spanish citizens were required to evacuate the city or declare loyalty to the British crown. Of the slightly more than 3,000 inhabitants, only eight remained. England divided the territory into two provinces, East Florida with St. Augustine as its capital, and West Florida with Pensacola as its capital.

• In 1764 the first governor, Colonel James Grant, arrived, and the two-hundred-year-old Spanish town began to acquire a British veneer.

• In 1764 the name of the Castillo de San Marcos was anglicized (changed) to Fort St. Marks.

• Starting in 1764 and during the ensuing years, the British began exporting indigo, lumber, oranges and naval stores. One of the large landowners, Lieutenant Governor John Moultrie, maintained residency both on his plantation (Bella Vista, south of town) and in his house in St. Augustine. Moultrie temporarily succeeded Grant as Governor when Grant returned to England.

• In 1764, to encourage settlement, as well as growth of agriculture products, the English government offered liberal grants of lands in Florida to English gentlemen of wealth and standing. Under this agreement Dr. Andrew Turnbull and associates of London secured a large tract of land eighty miles south of St. Augustine for the purpose of establishing a plantation colony. Turnbull named the place New Smyrna.

OLD CITY GATES, ST. AUGUSTINE, FLA.

31522

City Gate. All that now remains of the wall that, together with the moat, once protected St. Augustine on the north. Built by the Spaniards in 1743; it was rebuilt in 1804. Circa 1930s, $2-4.

• In 1767 Dr. Andrew Turnbull imported 1,400 people from the island of Minorca and relocated them to New Smyrna. For nine years these people worked on the plantations there, and then they revolted and obtained their freedom. The remaining colonists, some six hundred in number, settled in St. Augustine where their descendants are a large and thriving portion of the population at the present time.

• In 1775 the American Revolution began. Florida remained loyal to England.

• In 1779-81 St. Augustine-based troops helped defend Savannah against the French and Americans.

• In 1783 Florida was receded to Spain in exchange for the Bahama Islands and all the British population left in the country. Pathetic scenes of evacuation were repeated as most of the English residents left to seek new homes.

Second Spanish Period: 1783-1821

• In 1783 most of the houses in St. Augustine were made of stone or coquina. The many gardens in town were well stocked with fruit trees, such as figs, oranges, guavas, limes, and citrons.

• In 1783 a Spanish governor and garrison arrived to again occupy St. Augustine. With the return of Spanish rule, St. Augustine reverted to its former status as a military post, almost entirely dependent upon the Spanish government for support.

• In 1790 Spain allowed American settlers to immigrate into the Floridas.

• In 1812 under the leadership of General John H. McIntosh and calling themselves the Patriots, a number of American frontiersmen, Americans, banned themselves and attacked the Spaniards in Florida. They captured Fernandina, and with the aid of nine American gunboats, attacked St. Augustine. They also captured occupied Fort Mose, but were shelled out of it by a schooner; they failed to damage the town, the defenses of which were altogether too strong for them.

• In 1815 it became clear that Spain could no longer maintain her hold on Florida provinces.

• In 1819 a treaty was drafted, ceding Florida to the United States government. All that remained was ratification by the two nations involved, a process that took two long years.

Territorial Period and Early Statehood: 1821-1861

• In 1821 the flag of Spain gave way to the Stars and Stripes on the old fort. St. Augustine's long period under Spanish rule came to an end, and its period as a part of the United States began. At a colorful military ceremony on July 10, troops of the United States took possession of the territory and the Spanish soldiers departed, never to return again.

• In 1823 Tallahassee was selected as the capital. This was a compromise between St. Augustine and Pensacola.

The End of Spanish Rule. This celebration shows the change of flags on July 10, 1821, transferring St. Augustine to the United States. Circa 1940s, $6-8.

• In 1824 Congress ordered the name of the Castillo de San Marcos changed to Fort Marion.

• In 1832 the northeast section of Florida was the center of great activity. Several thriving plantations were producing great quantities of sugar, cotton, indigo, and rice.

• In 1836 the plantations in the vicinity of St. Augustine were attacked and burned, and refugees arrived with gory tales of Seminole Indian atrocities.

Fort Marion. Congress ordered the name of the Castillo de San Marcos changed to Fort Marion. Circa 1910s, $5-7.

• In 1835 the Seminole Indians were angry because the U. S. Government told them they had to move west of the Mississippi River to make room for white settlers. Many Seminoles, rather than move, decided to stay and fight. Before soldiers stopped them, the Seminoles burned and pillaged every white owned building they could find. This included the sugar plantations along Florida's East Coast. For eight years the bloody battles raged, until the Seminoles were either transported to the west or forced into seclusion in the Everglade swamps of South Florida. The Seminole War was the longest and bloodiest Indian conflict in American history.

• In 1835-42 the Seminole Indian War occurred. The war curtailed travel to St. Augustine. However, soldiers and officers from the North, who were stationed in the city, enlivened its social life and bolstered its economy. In their letters home they described the quaintness of the city and the beauty of its Minorcan girls.

A scene in the National Cemetery that shows the Major Dade Monument. In December 1835, Major Francis L. Dade and a detachment of 108 men left Fort Brooke (Tampa) for Fort King (Ocala). On the 28th, Seminole Indians ambushed the company; Major Dade and all but three of his men were killed. The dead from Major Dade's detachment were buried on the battlefield, but seven years later, their remains were relocated to the National Cemetery in St. Augustine where a memorial now stands. Cancelled 1910, $5-7.

• From 1836-42 the present sea wall was built by the United States Government, east of the old wall.

From 1836-1842, the government reconstructed the Sea Wall that was originally built by the Spanish in 1690. It extends from Castillo de San Marcos (Fort Marion) to the St. Francis Barracks. Shown in this view are the Sea Wall and Bath House. Cancelled 1909, $5-7.

• In 1836 Osceola, the patriot Seminole warrior, was captured under a flag of truce, and confined in Fort Marion along with Chiefs Coacoochee and Hadjo and other Seminole Indians. Osceola was later sent to Fort Moultrie in Charleston where he died in 1838.
• In 1836 Seminole Chiefs Caocoochee and Hadjo escaped from Fort Marion by squeezing through the iron bars and dropping into the fort's moat.
• In 1842 the Seminole War ended and Florida was safe once again for visitors, who among other reasons, came to take advantage of the fine climate.

Osceola, the most famous Seminole Indian, achieved lasting fame in American history when he chose death in prison rather than surrender to the United States authorities. He was the leader of the Seminoles during the Second Seminole War. He is pictured in this postcard view in a hunting skirt. A turban of red cloth with three ostrich plumes circles his head. Hanging from his neck are three silver gorgets that Osceola wore in all of his portraits. Circa 1993, $2-4.

- In 1845 Florida became the twenty-seventh state of the Union.
- In 1850 settlers were pushing into Central Florida while roads and railroads were being constructed to transport the state's agricultural produce.

The State Capitol in Tallahassee stands on a block-square knoll overlooking the business district. It was completed in 1845, the year Florida became a state, and since that time numerous additions have been made to the original building. Circa 1940s, $3-5.

- In 1855 many tourists visiting Florida participated in shooting alligators for sport.

Civil War Years and After: 1861-1880

- In 1861 on April 12 the Civil War began with a two-day bloodless bombardment of Fort Sumter in Charleston Harbor. The Civil War was the most traumatic experience in the history of the United States. Neither North nor South in 1861 could have envisioned the scope, or the horror, of that conflict. St. Augustine fared better than most southern towns; no troops stormed the city and no battles raged in nearby fields.
- In 1861 Florida seceded from the Union and the Confederates seized Fort Marion. The nation's oldest city remained a Confederate-held town for just over one year. While Florida never became a major theater of military operations, its production of salt, beef, pork, and other produce contributed to the Confederacy.
- In 1862 a Union assault force arrived off the coast of St. Augustine and requested the town's surrender. The offer was accepted and in short order the Stars and Stripes once again flew over Fort Marion. Unionists occupied and held St. Augustine until the end of the Civil War.
- In 1864 when the war ended, the people of St. Augustine could only breathe a sigh of relief. Houses had fallen into disrepair and the bridge over the San Sebastian River had been destroyed. Families grieved for the young men who would never return.
- In 1865, with the conclusion of the Civil War, St. Augustine was three hundred years old.
- In 1865, Yankees looking for a new location, ex-slaves and Southerners looking for new homes as far as possible from the conquerors streamed into Florida and St. Augustine with promises of land.

Florida Alligator Hunter

Hunting Alligators. In the 1800s many visitors to Florida amused themselves by shooting alligators from the deck of a steamboat. Even John J. Audubon, an early 19th century naturalist, found alligator hunting to be suitable entertainment for tourists. Regional guidebooks pointed out the best spots for alligator hunting. Commercial hunting and poaching became widespread throughout Florida as alligator skins became popular for a wide variety of leather items. Today, alligator hunting is controlled and alligators are plentiful throughout Florida. Cancelled 1913, $8-10.

• In 1871 steamboats on the St. Johns River stopped at Tocoi, fifty-three miles south of Jacksonville, to let off passengers who were traveling to St. Augustine. From Tocoi, passengers would board a horse or mule drawn railroad car for a short overland trip to the ancient city.

• In 1872 a Confederate Monument was placed in the Plaza de la Constitution.

• In 1875 a number of rebel Western Indians (Comanche, Kiowa and Arapaho) were confined in Fort Marion.

The Flagler Era: 1883-1899

• In 1883 the Jacksonville, St. Augustine and Halifax River Railway was completed, giving St. Augustine a link with neighbors to the north.

• In 1883 Henry Morrison Flagler and his new wife spent their honeymoon in St. Augustine and were introduced to the ancient city. A millionaire oil magnate, Flagler was compelled to return.

• In 1884 the War Department allocated funds to restore Fort Marion.

• In 1885 Flagler visited St. Augustine and was impressed with the luxury hotel, the San Marco. He was determined to build his own luxury hotel, which he would name the Ponce de Leon. St. Augustine's modern era began with the arrival of Flagler. He built a railroad and luxury hotel system along the East Coast of Florida.

• In 1886 five hundred Apache Indians crowded into Fort Marion. The Apaches, who were model prisoners, remained only a year. Army uniforms were issued to many of the Indians.

Steamboat travel to St. Augustine. St. Johns River steamboats stopped at Tocoi to let off passengers who were traveling to St. Augustine. From Tocoi, passengers would board a horse or mule drawn railroad car for a short 18-mile overland trip to the ancient city. Circa 1910s, $8-10.

Henry M. Flagler. In 1883, Henry M. Flagler, a retired Standard Oil Company executive, while visiting Florida on a holiday, realized that better transportation facilities were needed. From that point on, until his death in 1913, Flagler proceeded to help develop the East Coast of Florida. He built a railroad line, called the Florida East Coast Railway, from Jacksonville to Key West, and along the way, he developed a number of grand hotels that catered to wealthy tourists. His hotel chain started with the Ponce de Leon, Alcazar and Cordova hotels in St. Augustine. Circa 1910s, $3-5.

• In 1888 the Ponce de Leon Hotel opened its doors to winter visitors, with the Alcazar Hotel soon to follow. In the following year Henry M. Flagler bought the Casa Monica and renamed it the Cordova Hotel. From the day the Ponce de Leon opened its massive doors, the beautiful building dominated St. Augustine's center. The towers made the city's skyline unique and the whole structure, together with the Alcazar and Cordova, recreated Old Spain in the golden climate of northern Florida. When the hotels opened, St. Augustine became the foremost winter resort in America.

• In 1889 Flagler's dream was turning into an empire of hotels, resorts, railroads, churches, hospitals and many related businesses.

Ponce de Leon Hotel. In 1888, Henry M. Flagler built a resort hotel in St. Augustine that would rival the best hotels in the world. Many important visitors climbed the steps to the Ponce including five U. S. presidents. Circa 1930s, $3-5.

• In 1890 Flagler established the town of Hastings as an agricultural center to produce products for his hotels.

Hotel Hastings. Hastings, the Potato Capital of Florida located a few miles inland from St. Augustine, was founded in 1890 at the suggestion of Henry M. Flagler. Fifty men moved with their families into makeshift cabins on the new experimental plantation. A railroad was established, and the farm town began producing vegetables primarily for Flagler's St. Augustine hotels. The postcard depicts a 1900 view of the town. Circa 1910s, $8-10.

- In 1893 Felix Fire and George Reddington opened the St. Augustine Alligator Farm on Anastasia Island.
- In 1893 President and Mrs. Grover Cleveland visited St. Augustine.
- In 1895 a wooden bridge was erected to connect downtown St. Augustine with Anastasia Island.
- In 1897 it snowed in St. Augustine.

Twentieth Century and Beyond: 1900-Present

- In 1900 the "golden era" was starting to end, as Henry M. Flagler's interests moved south. His legacy, however, still remains in St. Augustine as his buildings grace the city as both monuments and architectural gems.
- In 1900 the country had just emerged from the Spanish American War for Cuban Independence. At this time transportation consisted of horse and buggy, railroads and steamboats.
- In 1900 the U. S. Army Post at Fort Marion was deactivated.
- In 1905 on October 21, President Roosevelt delivered a speech from the landing of the stairway in Fort Marion.
- In 1905 the remains of Volunteers of the Spanish American War were interred in the Military Cemetery.
- In 1906 Henry M. Flagler's mausoleum was built.

Alligators and St. Augustine. Alligators, a part of real Florida, may be found wherever there is a natural body of water. They are among the oldest, largest, and most advanced reptiles on earth. These prehistoric reptiles play an important role in the ecology of Florida's wetlands and are an important part of Florida's heritage. Alligators were here long before humans and have proved to be remarkably adaptable. An understanding of these facts and broader knowledge of alligator habits will ensure that humans and alligators continue their long-term coexistence. Alligators have always been a popular tourist attraction in St. Augustine. In 1893 the St. Augustine Alligator Farm opened on Anastasia Island and is still open. Circa 1910s, $8-10.

- In 1913, Henry Morrison Flagler died and was entombed in the mausoleum adjoining the Presbyterian Memorial Church where other members of his family already laid. St. Augustine reaped the benefits of Flagler's mighty empire.
- In 1920 and the decade to follow, the population of St. Augustine almost doubled, reaching more than 12,000.

Flagler's Mausoleum. Henry M. Flagler, builder of the East Coast of Florida, erected this church in 1889. Flagler and members of his family lie in the mausoleum, which is made of Italian marble. Circa 1940s, $2-4.

- In 1920 "tin lizzies" began to make an impact on St. Augustine.
- In 1924 Fort Marion and Fort Matanzas were proclaimed national monuments.
- In 1927 August Hecksher erected the elegant Vilano Beach Casino on a nearby ocean beach. St. Augustine's beaches were popular with locals as well as visitors. People were ferried across the Matanzas River to pavilions and bathhouses to enjoy good food, fun and a dip in the ocean.
- In 1929 a coquina sphere six feet in diameter, called the zero milestone, was placed between Bay Street and the City Gate. It marks the eastern terminus of an old trail that linked the Spanish missions between St. Augustine and Pensacola.

Florida or Bust. Highways began to reach St. Augustine before the 1920s and by the time these families packed into their motorcars and took to the road, there were hard-surface highways to take the adventurous all around Florida. The cartoon shown on this postcard appeared in the November 26, 1925 issue of Life magazine. Circa 1920s, $3-5.

• In 1935 the potbellied boats of the shrimp fleet played an important part in a popular industry in St. Augustine. Shrimp were iced and canned and were to be sent to northern markets. These boats can best be viewed from the King Street Bridge over the San Sebastian River.

Shrimp Boats in Port. Shrimping plays an important part as an industry in St. Augustine, this popular seafood being plentiful in local waters. At one time the shrimp boat fleet was composed of 123 documented vessels. Shrimp are iced, as well as canned, to be sent to northern markets. Circa 1940s, $3-5.

• In 1938 Marineland, Florida's first aquatic attraction, opened along the Atlantic Ocean, eighteen miles south of St. Augustine Beach.
• In 1942 Congress restored the fort's original Spanish name, Castillo de San Marcos.
• In 1945, St. Augustine, weathering the storm of World War II, underwent a face lift that returned the city to the appearance of the first Spanish period. As a result of this, St. Augustine again became a major point of interest for tourists.

Marineland of Florida, home of educated porpoises, is located on the coastal highway, eighteen miles south of St. Augustine Beach. It is the world's first oceanarium and studio designed for professional underwater motion picture photography. The performing porpoises and whales of Marineland have been delighting visitors since 1938, but Marineland has been a center for the scientific study of marine biology as well as entertainment for visitors. Circa 1950s, $3-5.

• In 1946 Casper's Ostrich and Alligator Farm opened two miles north of St. Augustine on U.S. Highway 1.

This postcard shows an animal trainer performing with an alligator at Casper's Ostrich and Alligator Farm in St. Augustine. Circa 1940s, $3-5.

- In 1950 railroad travel was in decline and most people visiting St. Augustine came by automobile.
- In 1955 and beyond, there was an ongoing effort to preserve and restore many colonial structures in St. Augustine.
- In 1959 the St. Augustine Historical Restoration and Preservation Commission was established with the responsibility of acquiring, restoring and preserving certain ancient or historic landmarks, buildings, sites, and other objects of historical interest of the city.

- In 1965 St. Augustine was 400 years old.

- In 2007 St. Augustine has a historic district of 144 blocks on the National Register of Historic Places. It is here we find the oldest examples of almost everything in the United States: the oldest house, the oldest wooden schoolhouse, the oldest military fort, the oldest store, the oldest jail, the oldest alligator farm, etc.

Automobile Travel. After 1950 railroad travel was in decline and most visitors to St. Augustine came by automobile. Circa 1940s, $2-4.

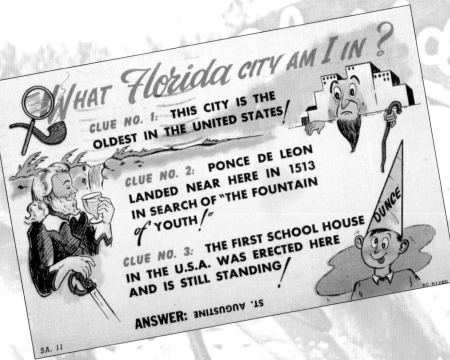

Where Am I? A comical postcard about St. Augustine. Cancelled 1952, $3-5.

Chapter Three

Around Town: City and Street Views

A postcard view of a tree-lined King Street as it appeared in the early 1900s. The Ponce de Leon Hotel can be seen in the distance. Several historic structures are located on this popular street, including the Ponce de Leon Hotel (now Flagler College), Alcazar Hotel (now Lightner Museum), Cordova Hotel (now Casa Monica Hotel), Government House Museum, Potter's Wax Museum, Villa Zorayda (now Zorayda Castle) and the south side of the Plaza de la Constitution. The Plaza de la Constitution was created in the sixteenth century by royal decree and required that all Spanish colonial towns be built around a central plaza. It functioned as the principal recreational and meeting area in the heart of the community. Circa 1904, $6-8.

King Street, St. Augustine, Fla.

Narrow Streets of St. Augustine. Like all Spanish towns in this hemisphere, St. Augustine was laid out on a specific grid pattern prescribed by royal ordinance. Street widths were between twelve and twenty-two feet and the crossing lanes eight feet wide. According to a diary describing St. Augustine in 1765, "the town was pleasantly situated but without regularity. Ye streets are very narrow… and almost all houses are built after ye Spanish fashion with pleasant covered balconies… as well as garden and yard walls…" This early 1900s postcard view shows several horse-drawn carriages on King Street, one of the primary streets in St. Augustine. Postmarked 1909, $6-8.

Old Charlotte Street, St. Augustine, Florida.

The Oldest City in the United States

60876

Charlotte Street. St. Augustine's Spanish colonial origin is reflected in its architecture and narrow streets. Charlotte Street, one of the main thoroughfares of the city, is especially interesting because of the number of old dwellings it contains. The early Spanish residences were built of coquina, and many of them were provided with balconies projecting from the second stories; the narrowness of the streets rendered the latter feature a great aid to neighborly sociability. Circa 1920s, $1-3.

"Street that leads to the Barracks," later named Charlotte Street, was one of the four lines of travel north and south of the ancient military city within the fortifications. St. Augustine retains much of its old time characteristics in some sections. General Hernandez, who captured the famous Seminole Indian, Osceola, lived on this street. Circa 1915, $1-3.

CHARLOTTE STREET.

This postcard shows a westward view of Cathedral Street from the Sea Wall. Shown is the Farmers' Market to the left and the Ponce de Leon Hotel in the distance.
Circa 1914, $4-6.

Aviles Street, Old Spanish Quarter

Aviles Street. Along this narrow, picturesque street are some of St. Augustine's most historic houses, as well as many interesting shops. The Old Public Library, Ximenez-Fatio House, Don Toledo House, and others give this street its special character. The original name of Aviles Street was Hospital Street. It is the shortest street in St. Augustine (.2 of a mile long). Circa 1920s, $1-3.

This postcard shows the historic and romantic Aviles Street with a horse drawn carriage being operated by a careful guide. Aviles Street was named after Pedro Menendez de Aviles, the city's founder. Circa 1940s, $1-3.

St. George Street is the main artery in St. Augustine. Today it courses through the heart of San Agustin Antiquo, the restored eighteenth century Spanish colonial village. The old City Gate is shown at the far end of this view. This street was originally called, by the Spanish, "the street to the City Gate." The Spanish generally named their streets by destination. Circa 1915, $1-3.

The Old City Gate consists of two square pillars of coquina rock, twenty feet in height. The space between the pillars is twelve feet and was protected with a heavy iron bound gate. This view is looking through the pillars toward St. George Street. Circa 1915, $2-4.

This postcard is of St. George Street at the intersection of Cathedral Street and shows the corner Post Office, Catholic residence and a few prominent business places located on this busy thoroughfare. Cancelled 1916, $5-7.

ST. AUGUSTINE, Fla. Treasury Street, the Narrowest Street in the U.S.

Treasury Street. This narrow street stretches between Bay Street (now Avenida Menendez) and Cordova Street. The street is still a popular tourist site. Cancelled 1909, $6-8.

Treasury St., Narrowest Street in United States, 7 Feet Wide 8

St. Augustine, Florida The Oldest City in the United States

Treasury Street has the dubious distinction of being the narrowest street in the city, barely reaching a seven-foot width in some sections. It was once used as a roadway during the Spanish period. Circa 1930s, $1-3.

The Narrowest Street in the United States, St. Augustine, Florida

Another view of Treasury Street. Circa 1940s, $2-4.

This is a hand painted postcard of an 1874 engraving that shows the Oldest House on the right. Cancelled 1954, $2-4.

Bay Street. A walk along the seawall was a pleasant diversion in the early 1900s. On the right, Capo's Bath House stands ready for bathers. Bay Street is now named Avenida Menendez. Circa 1910, $4-6.

Chapter Four

Crossing The Matanzas River: Bridges

Seawall and South Beach Bridge, St. Augustine, Fla.

An early 1900s postcard view of the South Beach Bridge. This wooden bridge remained operational until it was replaced with the Bridge of Lions on April 7, 1927. Tourists could ride the rail car across the bridge to attractions on Anastasia Island (Lighthouse, Whitney's Burning Spring Museum, Alligator Farm, and Watchtower Ruins). Cancelled 1911, $12-14.

The Matanzas River, part of the East Coast Intercoastal Waterway, flows under the Bridge of Lions. Circa 1940s, $1-3.

Completed by the people of St. Augustine in 1927, the Bridge of Lions connects the quaint old city with Anastasia Island and St. Augustine Beach, a fifteen mile stretch of Atlantic Ocean coastline. The concrete structure with drawbridge and towers spans the Matanzas River. Two huge lions, from which the bridge takes its name, stand at the entrance to the span. These lions of white Italian marble were a gift to the city by Dr. Andrew Anderson, a close friend of Henry M. Flagler. Circa 1930s, $1-3.

This aerial view shows the Castello de San Marcos, several shrimp boats and the Bridge of Lions crossing the Matanzas River. Circa 1945, $1-3.

Bridge Of Lions. This is one of the most beautiful bridges along Florida's Intercoastal Waterway. It's a classic 1920s design, with clean lines and red-roofed bridge towers. Stately marble lions, balancing their paws on spheres, guard each end of the bridge. Circa 1930s, $1-3.

Chapter Five

Visiting In Town: Hotels

Bird's Eye View of Alcazar and Cordova Hotels from the Ponce de Leon, St. Augustine, Fla.
Noted for their Spanish and Moorish Architecture.

This postcard shows a bird's-eye view of Flagler's hotels, the Cordova and Alcazar from the Ponce de Leon, in 1893. Henry M. Flagler fell in love with St. Augustine on his first visit in 1883. He built two luxurious hotels, the Ponce de Leon and the Alcazar, and acquired the Cordova. For the convenience of wealthy winter visitors, he extended train service (on the Florida East Coast Railway) to what was being heralded as the "Newport of the South." The Ponce de Leon, located on King Street, was a luxury hotel. The Alcazar across the street was less formal and less expensive than its dramatic neighbor. The Casa Monica Hotel was built by Franklin W. Smith at the time Flagler's hotels were under construction, but within a year it was renamed the Cordova when Flagler bought it. Circa 1915, $4-6.

This postcard shows the Ponce de Leon Hotel as seen from the Cordova Hotel. The Ponce was one of the state's architectural treasures and a centerpiece of activity in St. Augustine. Circa 1907, $6-8.

St. Augustine, Fla. The Ponce De Leon fr
The Co

Front Entrance to Ponce de Leon Hotel, St. Augustine, Fla.

The grandeur, furnishings and landscaping of the Ponce de Leon reflected the artistry of architects James A. McGuire and Joseph E. McDonald, and the touch of Henry M. Flagler's millions. It had two miles of corridors and covered most of a five-acre lot. The exterior walls of the hotel, four feet thick, were made of poured concrete. The furnishings in each of the 450 rooms and suites were worth about $1,000, which was a great deal of money in the 1880s. Circa 1910, $2-6.

Front and Main Entrance. Facing south from this doorway offered a full view of the magnificence of the courtyard. The doorway opened into the rotunda of the hotel from the court. Circa 1910, $4-6.

Ponce de Leon Hotel. Built at a cost of $2.5 million, this hotel of Spanish style architecture opened in 1888. It was one of the famous East Coast System hostelries and considered to be one of the finest hotels in the world. It has five acres of roof. Circa 1920s, $1-3.

A court view of the Ponce. The main parlor of the magnificent Ponce de Leon Hotel is 104 by 53 feet; the dining room measures 150 by 90 feet and seats 500 guests; the rotunda is four stories high with arcades and galleries at each story; the court is filled with beautiful tropical flora. Circa 1910, $2-4.

LOGIA OF HOTEL PONCE DE LEON, ST. AUGUSTINE, FLA.

70210   THE COURT OF THE PONCE DE LEON, ST. AUGUSTINE, FLA.   COPR. DETROIT PUBLISHING CO.

The roofed-open gallery of the Ponce de Leon was a favorite lounging place for guests during concert performances in the court. The wide-arched verandas flanked the courtyard. Circa 1915, $1-3.

Tourists relax in the courtyard of the opulent Ponce de Leon Hotel in 1905. The vine-clad verandas were surrounded by handsomely landscaped grounds. Circa 1920, $4-6.

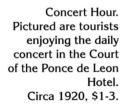

Concert Hour. Pictured are tourists enjoying the daily concert in the Court of the Ponce de Leon Hotel. Circa 1920, $1-3.

CONCERT HOUR, COURT OF PONCE DE LEON HOTEL, ST. AUGUSTINE, FLA.

Carriage entrance to the Ponce de Leon Hotel. Circa 1910, $3-5.

The Alcazar Hotel, built in 1888, occupied an entire square on the opposite side of King Street from the Ponce de Leon Hotel. It was designed in Spanish renaissance style, with courts, fountains, gardens, and running water. Though smaller, it was considered as beautiful as the Ponce de Leon. Today, the structure is used as the Lightner Museum. Circa 1910, $3-5.

Court entrance to the Ponce de Leon Hotel. The entrance was flanked by heraldic lion heads, a symbol of the Spanish town of Leon. Cancelled 1914, $3-5.

This postcard shows the Alcazar Court looking through to King Street. Adaptions from famous Moorish buildings in Spain were incorporated into the Alcazar, which blended beautifully with its garden settings. The great central court, which was one mass of foliage, was in view as hotel visitors dined. Circa 1908, $4-6.

The front towers of the Alcazar Hotel. Circa 1910, $4-6.

The courtyard was one of the picturesque features of the Alcazar Hotel. Circa 1910s, $1-3.

Indoor Swimming. The Alcazar Hotel swimming pool was once the largest indoor swimming pool in the world. Cancelled 1924, $3-5.

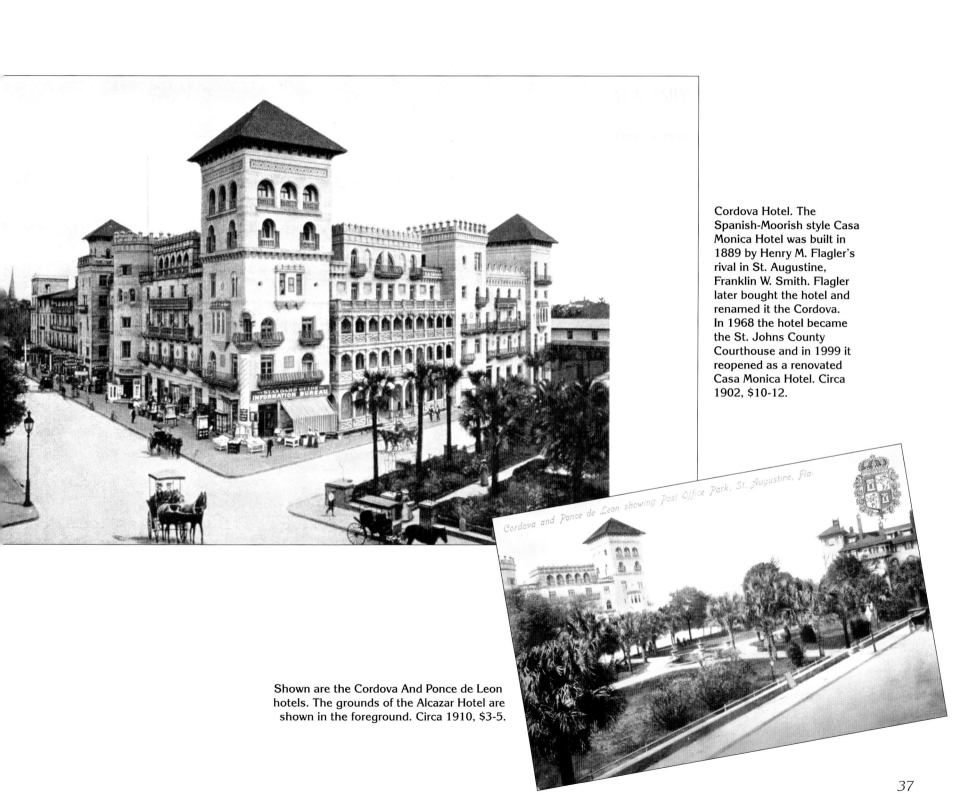

Cordova Hotel. The Spanish-Moorish style Casa Monica Hotel was built in 1889 by Henry M. Flagler's rival in St. Augustine, Franklin W. Smith. Flagler later bought the hotel and renamed it the Cordova. In 1968 the hotel became the St. Johns County Courthouse and in 1999 it reopened as a renovated Casa Monica Hotel. Circa 1902, $10-12.

Cordova and Ponce de Leon showing Post Office Park, St. Augustine, Fla.

Shown are the Cordova And Ponce de Leon hotels. The grounds of the Alcazar Hotel are shown in the foreground. Circa 1910, $3-5.

Magnolia Hotel was one of the oldest and most popular hotels in St. Augustine. It was built in 1847 by B.E. Carr and was located on St. George Street at the corner of Hypolita Street. Circa 1910s, $5-7.

Castle Warden Hotel. The St. Augustine winter home of a Standard Oil Company magnate, the Castle Warden was constructed of poured concrete in the 1880s. Norton Baskin acquired the structure and ran it as the Castle Warden Hotel. In 1950, Ripley's Believe It Or Not converted it into a museum. Circa 1930s, $3-5.

Another view of the Magnolia Hotel. Circa 1910s, $3-5.

The St. George Hotel, located on the corner of St. George Street and the Plaza, was only a few steps from the Ponce de Leon, the Cathedral, the Bay, etc. Circa 1908, $8-10.

In 1892, the St. George Hotel was advertised as the most attractive family hotel in "Ye Ancient Citie." Circa 1915, $3-5.

A real photo postcard taken with a hotel guest's camera of the St. George Hotel. Cancelled 1913, $8-10.

The Spear Mansion Hotel had accommodations for 100 guests. Circa 1910, $3-5.

The Florida House was described in 1848 as "a large well-kept establishment belonging to Mr. Cole." In 1892 the rates for transient guests was $3 to $4 per day. Circa 1910, $4-6.

The Buckingham Hotel was located directly opposite the Ponce de Leon and Alcazar hotels. It had beautiful grounds, large verandas and sun parlors. Hand colored card. Circa 1910, $5-7.

The Buckingham   St. Augustine, Florida

Granada Hotel was a picturesque structure at the corner of King and Granada streets, facing the Alameda. It had accommodations for about 200 guests and featured its own pigeon loft, poultry, dairy and vegetable farms. Cancelled 1911, $8-10.

ST. AUGUSTINE, Fla. Hotel Granada.

Another view of
the Granada Hotel.
Cancelled 1907, $8-10.

Hotel Granada, St. Augustine, Fla.

S. A. 140—Hotel Monson, Saint Augustine, Fla.

The Monson Hotel was erected on Bay
Street (now Avenida Menendez) to
replace the original Monson House, a late
nineteenth century wooden structure. The
hotel, built after the 1914 fire destroyed its
predecessor, was razed in the 1960s. The
Monson Riverfront Inn now occupies the
site. Circa 1930, $2-4.

Monson Hotel was located on Matanzas Bay, overlooking the Atlantic Ocean. Circa 1930, $4-6.

The Bennett Hotel had elegant steam heated rooms with or without private baths, electric elevators, and private sunny piazzas overlooking the bay and ocean. Circa 1920s, $5-7.

The Bennett Hotel was located on Bay Street (now Avenida Menendez) overlooking Matanzas Bay. The towers of the Castillo de San Marcos can be seen in the distance and two horse-drawn carriages are shown in this early 1900s postcard view. Circa 1930s, $1-3.

Marion Hotel was located on beautiful Matanzas Bay and had a homey atmosphere. Circa 1930s, $2-4.

The Barcelona Hotel was located at the corner of Carrera and Sevilla streets. Circa 1930s, $2-4.

Plaza Hotel and Potter's Wax Museum. The only hotel in St. Augustine located on Matanzas Bay and the Plaza. The Potter's Wax Museum is located in the same building. This museum brings to life the great figures of ancient and modern-world history and features over 150 sculpted figures. Circa 1930s, $7-9.

Hotels along the Bay. Guests staying at these shoreline hotels had an excellent view of Matanzas Bay. Circa 1908, $4-6.

Chapter Six

Government Business

The Old Spanish Treasury, St. Augustine, Fla.

34

The Oldest City in the United States

60736

The Old Spanish Treasury on St. George Street was once the residence of the Royal Treasurer, Juan Esteban de Pena (1740-1763). A second floor was added in 1838 by Dr. Seth S. Peck. In 1912, Anna G. Burt, granddaughter of Dr. Peck, inherited the property and bequeathed it in 1931 to the City of St. Augustine. The structure is now known as the Pena-Peck House. Circa 1930s, $1-3.

Court House, St. Augustine, Fla.

Court House. In June 1907, St. Johns County officials moved into a new courthouse built at Charlotte and Treasury streets. The building of Spanish architecture had a very ornate exterior, with a wide hall extending the length of the building and offices opening off it. The structure cost $55,000. Circa 1908, $10-12.

St. Augustine, Fla. Post Office from Plaza

Shown is the old Spanish Governor's Palace when it was used as a Post Office. Cancelled 1908, $5-7.

Court House. On April 2, 1914, a fire that began in the nearby Florida House spread to the courthouse, destroying it. A new courthouse was built in 1918 at the same location. Circa 1908, $8-10.

This Post Office building replaced the old Spanish Governor's Palace, which was used as an earlier post office. Circa 1930s, $1-3.

United States Post Office. St. Augustine, Fla.

The Oldest City in the United States

Post Office and Ponce de Leon Hotel Towers. This postcard view, looking west on Cathedral Place from St. George Street, shows the "Horse and Buggy" so popular with tourists for sight-seeing trips within the city. Circa 1940s, $1-3.

From 1834 the Post Office was located on one of the most historic properties in St. Augustine, "Government House," a leading administrative center since at least 1598. The site has been the location of the Spanish governors' residence, the Federal Building, and, since 1966, the main offices of the Historical St. Augustine Preservation Board and the Government House Museum. Circa 1930s, $1-3.

The Civic Center contained an auditorium seating nine hundred people and club rooms for tourists. Today it is used as the Visitor Information Center. Cancelled 1941, $1-3.

Chapter Seven
Oldest House In America

Gonzalez-Alvarez House. For more than three centuries this site has been occupied. This coquina stone house was built soon after the English burned St. Augustine in 1702. As times changed during the Spanish, British and American occupations, a wooden second story, an off-street porch, and other features were added. Cancelled 1907, $3-5.

Photo, only, Copyright 1904 by the Rotograph Co.
G 15023 Old House, St. Francis Street, St. Augustine, Fla.

OLDEST HOUSE IN THE U. S., ST. FRANCIS ST., ST. AUGUSTINE, FLA.

The Gonzalez-Alvarez House, known as the "Oldest House," is one of the country's most-studied and best documented old houses. For more than a hundred years after St. Augustine's founder, Pedro Menendez de Aviles, landed in 1565, the little community was repeatedly raided and burned by the English and pirates. Yet, despite those dark days of violence, the site of the Oldest House has been continuously occupied by Europeans and Americans since the 1600s. Circa 1920s, $1-3.

Oldest House. In 1911, George Reddington, one of the founders of the St. Augustine Alligator Farm, purchased the Alvarez House on St. Francis Street. Reddington held the property for seven years, selling it in 1918 to the St. Augustine Historical Society, which continues to exhibit the building. It became a registered National Landmark in 1970. Circa 1930s, $1-3.

Oldest House, St. Francis Street

Sightseeing via "Horse and Buggy"

PATIO, SHOWING WISHING WELL, OLDEST HOUSE IN THE U.S. FROM LOGGIA OF WEBB MEMORIAL BUILDING

Banks of beautiful flowers and tropical foliage in the patio add the colors of the rainbow to enhance the beauty of this historical house. The Oldest House is famous throughout the nation as a show place rich in historical tradition. Circa 1920s, $1-3.

This postcard shows the four flags that have flown over St. Augustine (Spanish, English, American, and Confederate). Circa 1940s, $1-3.

OLDEST HOUSE GARDEN, ST. AUGUSTINE, FLORIDA—89K

Garden at the Oldest House. Fruit bearing trees similar to those planted by the town's earliest settlers are in the gardens alongside the restored house. Small vegetable gardens are tended to with tools similar to those used in the eighteenth century. Circa 1930s, $1-3.

The Oldest House, on St. Francis Street, is a two-story, vine-clad structure with hip roof and stands flush with the street. The first story has very thick walls of coquina blocks; the second story is of wood, with a covered balcony at each end. The interior is impressive with cedar beams and very large fireplaces. A restoration was made in 1888 along with a tower. Circa 1920s, $1-3.

Upstairs Bedroom in the Oldest House. In the American Territorial Period this style of bedroom was popular. It exhibits the bed of General Hernandez, a famous leader in the war against the Seminole Indians. Circa 1930s, $2-4.

Main Room in the Oldest House. Tomas Gonzalez, an artillery man at the Castillo de San Marcos, lived here with his family in 1727. The Gonzalez family abandoned the house in 1763 to the British who had then taken over Florida. The next tenant was Major Joseph Peavett, a wealthy Englishman. Circa 1930s, $2-4.

Fireplace in the Oldest House. The stark interior of the Oldest House conveys the simplicity of life in the seventeenth century. Circa 1920s, $1-3.

Chapter Eight

Where They Lived: Residences

At one time, the Worth House on Marine Street was thought to be the oldest house in St. Augustine. Several very old houses, built within a few years of each other, are located in St. Augustine. Circa 1910s, $3-5.

Houses on Charlotte Street. The structures shown in this postcard were examples of St. Augustine houses during the first Spanish occupation (1565-1763). Circa 1950s, $1-3.

At one time, the Whitney House on Hospital Street (now Aviles Street) was thought to be the oldest house in St. Augustine. Circa 1907, $5-7.

Fatio House

This structure at 20 Aviles Street was constructed in 1798 by Spanish merchant Andres Ximenez. Louisa Fatio acquired the building in 1855 and was one of a long line of women who operated it as a boarding house. The building is known as the Ximenez-Fatio House. The house and its separate kitchen have been restored and furnished as an 1850 boarding house. It is owned by the National Society of Colonial Dames of America in the State of Florida. Circa 1930s, $3-5.

OLD DON TOLEDO HOUSE, ST. AUGUSTINE, FLORIDA

Located on Aviles Street is the Don Toledo House, a Spanish residence of the period between 1783 and 1821. The square house is two stories high with a gently sloping gable roof and is built of coquina blocks; it has wide windows and a projecting balcony. There is a quantity of antique furniture and curios on display. Circa 1920s, $1-3.

OLD HOUSE OF DON TOLEDO, AVILES STREET, ST. AUGUSTINE, FLA.

Another view of the Don Toledo House. Circa 1920s, $1-3.

The Moorish Revival style "Villa Zorayda" was built by architect Franklin W. Smith in 1883 for his winter residence. It was the first poured concrete structure in St. Augustine and launched a revolution in architectural style and construction technique, which was adopted by Henry M. Flagler in the building of his Ponce de Leon and Alcazar hotels. Today this structure is known as Zorayda Castle. Circa 1930s, $1-3.

The Vedder Collection of ancient maps and relics was exhibited by Nicholas Vedder in this Bay Street (now Avenida Menendez) building on the corner of Treasury Street. The coquina structure was the former residence of John Leslie, owner of a trading firm operating during the British and Second Spanish regimes. The structure and its contents were consumed by flames in 1914. Circa 1910s, $3-5.

The coquina and yellow brick Villa Flora, located at 234 St. George Street, was built in 1898 by Rev. O. A. Weenolsen as a "winter cottage." It is one of the few buildings in St. Augustine that has an above-ground basement. At one time it was credited with being the most beautiful residence in St. Augustine. Circa 1910s, $1-3.

The Llambias House was owned at one time by Nicholas Turnbull, the son of Dr. Andrew Turnbull, the founder of New Smyrna. The house later became the property of Minorcans and their descendants and eventually to Catalina Usina Llambias. Several Llambias children were born in the house. Circa 1940s, $1-3.

The Casa Ribera was reconstructed on its original massive archaeological foundation by St. Augustine Restoration, Inc. It depicts the home of a prosperous Spanish resident on the eighteenth century colonial Calle Rest (now St. George Street). Behind the plain wall is a stunning Spanish garden. Copyright 1983, $1-3.

OLD CURIOSITY SHOP, ST. GEORGE STREET.

Shown in this postcard view is the "Old Curiosity Shop" at 54 St. George Street. Built as a home in the early 1800s, it has been preserved and its walled garden restored by the St. Augustine Historical Society. Circa 1920, $1-3.

ST. FRANCIS ST., ST. AUGUSTINE, FLA., SHOWING OLDEST HOUSE IN DISTANCE.

In the first house on the left, the Tovar House, a historic Spanish building, a solid shot was found embedded in the walls. It was fired from General Oglethorpe's battery, located on Anastasia Island, in the siege of St. Augustine in 1740. The infantryman Jose Tovar lived on this corner in 1763. The house remained unchanged through the British Period (1763-1783) when the Scottish merchant John Johnson, lived here. Later occupant/owners of the house were Jose Coruna, Thomas Caraballo, and Geronimo Alvarez. The Tovar House has been owned by the St. Augustine Historical Society since 1918. Circa 1930, $2-4.

Chapter Nine
Oldest Schoolhouse In America

The Oldest School House in America, located on quaint St. George Street, was built prior to 1763. It has been a tourist attraction since 1931. Circa 1930s, $1-3.

Located near the City Gate, the Old School House is a surviving expression of another time. Built over two hundred years ago while Florida was under the rule of Spain, it was constructed of red cedar and cypress and put together with wooden pegs and handmade nails. Circa 1920s, $1-3.

The Oldest School House, St. George Street, St. Augustine, Florida

OLDEST SCHOOL HOUSE

The Oldest City in the United States

Oldest School House. Built as a residence, it was used early on as a school. Old Spanish kitchen in the garden is of special interest. Maps of the first Spanish occupation as well as the timeworn beams and planks of the building attest to the antiquity of this house. Circa 1930s, $1-3.

The Oldest School House in the U. S. A., St. Augustine, Florida 241

This view of the Oldest School House shows the plants, flowers and vines that surround the house. Circa 1930s, $1-3.

Another view of the Oldest School House. Circa 1940s, $1-3.

Garden at the Oldest School House. The Old Wooden School House is a vine-covered building of cedar and cypress with a stone chimney. One of its most interesting features is the original kitchen. Circa 1930s, $1-3.

The schoolmaster and his wife lived upstairs, above the small (and oldest) classroom. Their kitchen was separated from the main building because of the threat of fire and to spare the house of any excess heat during the long summers. Circa 1930s, $2-4.

Chapter Ten

America's Oldest Fort: Castillo de San Marcos

Castillo de San Marcos. This ancient fortress was built by the Spanish beginning in 1672; it has successfully defended St. Augustine against all attackers. The Castillo, as well as the City of St. Augustine, is a reminder of the Spanish Territories in the New World. Circa 1940s, $1-3.

The Oldest City in the United States

Castillo de San Marcos. The fort's 16-foot thick walls are built of coquina, a natural shellrock quarried on nearby Anastasia Island. The Castillo withstood major English attacks in 1702 and 1740, and was declared a National Monument in 1924. It is run by the National Park Service and is one of Florida's most important historic monuments. Circa 1930s, $1-3.

A bird's-eye view of St. Augustine from a watch tower at the Castillo de San Marcos. Cancelled 1907, $1-3.

THE CHANGE OF FLAGS ~ JULY 10TH 1821

Change Of Flags. The Castillo and Florida came into American hands through a treaty signed with Spain in 1821. On July 10th, the Spanish flag came down for the last time, and the twenty-three starred flag of the United States rose over the old embattlements. In 1824 Congress ordered the name of the Castillo changed to Fort Marion. This was to honor General Francis Marion of South Carolina, known as the famous "Swamp Fox" of the Revolutionary War. During the Civil War, the Confederate flag flew over Fort Marion for just over one year until 1862 when Union forces held St. Augustine until the end of the Civil War. In 1941, Congress restored the fort's original Spanish name, Castillo de San Marcos. Circa 1940s, $6-8.

An early 1900s view of the Castello de San Marcos (Fort Marion). It is one of the few links on this continent to early modern Europe methods of warfare, which has become obsolete. Cancelled 1908, $1-3.

Main Entrance to Fort. The Castillo de San Marcos was built to protect the Spanish settlements and Spanish Treasure fleets. The Castillo survived two major sieges and was never captured by an enemy during battle. The fort has walls 21 feet high, a moat that surrounded it, bastions on the corners, heavy casemates, dungeons and subterranean passages. Cancelled 1909, $3-5.

An aerial view of the fort. Cancelled 1912, $2-4.

Old Watch Tower. St. Augustine was Spain's Atlantic outpost in North America. From the fort's watch tower, the sentries watched out toward the inlet and the sea. This postcard, mailed in 1910, shows a watch tower at the Castillo. Cancelled 1910, $5-7.

St. Augustine, Fla. Interior Court Yard, Fort Marion, showing Entrance to old Chapel.

Courtyard. Beautifully arched casemates and interesting cornices testify to the workmanship and imagination of the Spanish builders. The fort contains guardrooms, dungeons, living quarters for the garrison, storerooms and a chapel. Nearly all the rooms open on a court, about a hundred feet square. Circa 1910s, $1-3.

Stairway and Roman Arch, Fort Marion, St. Augustine, Fla.

Courtyard And Ramp. The angled stairway led to the fort's "gun deck." The fort would accommodate a garrison of 1,000 men and 100 guns. Circa 1907, $3-5.

Sergeant Brown, shown at the chapel door, was for many years in charge of Ft. Marion. Circa 1910s, $1-3.

Interior of Fort Marion, (Doorway with Sergeant Brown,) St. Augustine, Fla.

SA.91—The Ramp to the Gun Deck
Castillo de San Marcos National Monument
St. Augustine, Fla.

Spanish soldiers and their heavy equipment moved quickly up this ramp to the "fighting deck" on top of the fort. The steps were added in modern times for visitor safety. The supporting arch, though unusual in this country, is typical of Spanish military architecture in the 1700s. Circa 1930s, $1-3.

St. Augustine, Fla., from Watch Tower of Fort Marion.

A view of the Gun Deck from a watch tower.
Circa 1910s, $1-3.

St. Augustine, Fla., Water Battery, Fort San Marco.

Each corner of the Castillo is protected by a diamond-shaped bastion. From the bastion the adjacent walls could be protected from an attacking force, and in conjunction with the neighboring bastions, a deadly cross fire could be turned on any force that got so close. The bastions provided the cross fire necessary to protect the main walls. Circa 1905, $3-5.

The moat was dry and used to keep livestock during times of attack. This dry moat served as a major obstacle to infantry attacking the Castillo. The National Park Service had water in the moat from 1938-1996. The water was removed to insure the structural integrity of the fort. The moat and towers of the massive fort helped it withstand many assaults. Circa 1980s, $1-3.

Florida. Watch Tower and Moat, Ft. Marion, St. Augustine

Watch Tower And Moat. Cancelled 1911, $2-4.

Seminole Room. A casemate at Fort Marion displaying a scene where Osceola has just returned from a hunt. This display was presented to the Historical Society by the Hon. Chauncey M. Depew. Circa 1920s, $2-4.

SEMINOLE ROOM, FORT MARION, ST. AUGUSTINE, FLA.   80364

An important service of the fort was as a military prison. Those imprisoned here were Seminoles in 1837-38, Plains Indians in 1875-78, Apaches in 1886-87, and Army deserters during the Spanish-American War. In October, 1837, almost a hundred of Florida's Seminole Indians were captured under a white flag of truce just south of St. Augustine. Included in the group were the famous warriors Osceola and Caocoochee. Most of these prisoners spent six weeks locked up at Fort Marion. Twenty of the prisoners, among them Caocoochee, staged an escape on the night of November 29, 1837, and carried on the fighting. Soon after, Osceola (shown in the above postcard view) was moved to Fort Moultrie in Charleston, South Carolina where he died on January 30, 1838. Use of Fort Marion ended in 1900, when the Army withdrew its troops from St. Augustine. Circa 1920s, $2-4.

CHIEF OSCEOLA OF THE SEMINOLES CONFINED IN COURT ROOM.

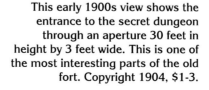

FORT MARION, ST. AUGUSTINE, FLA.

IN THE DUNGEONS, FORT MARION, ST. AUGUSTINE, FLA.
COPYRIGHT 1904 BY W. J. HARRIS.

This early 1900s view shows the entrance to the secret dungeon through an aperture 30 feet in height by 3 feet wide. This is one of the most interesting parts of the old fort. Copyright 1904, $1-3.

GUARD ROOM AND DUNGEON, FORT MARION, ST. AUGUSTINE, FLA.

Guard Room and Dungeon Entrance. This dungeon was used for confinement of prisoners for minor offenses. Circa 1910s, $1-3.

HOT SHOT OVEN, FORT MARION, ST. AUGUSTINE, FLA.

Hot Shot Oven. In this oven shot (cannon balls) were heated to fire at wooden vessels. At the rear may be seen bullet holes in the wall where prisoners were executed. Circa 1920s, $1-3.

THE FAMOUS SECRET DUNGEON, FORT MARION, ST. AUGUSTINE, FLA.
COPYRIGHT 1904 BY W. J. HARRIS

Secret Dungeon. This view shows the original gunpowder magazine that was later dubbed a "secret dungeon." The sun never shined in this room. Copyright 1904, $1-3.

A view of the hot shot oven and watch tower. Circa 1910s, $1-3.

A view of the fort from a watch tower. The Castillo took 23 years to build and cost more than 138,000 pesos ($218,360). The design of the fort is "stellar." It has a square central courtyard with a series of storage rooms around it with diamond-shaped bastions at each corner. Cancelled 1914, $2-4.

Old Spanish Door. Shown on this door is the last one of the original Spanish locks, which was first locked, and then a large bolt with a hasp closed the first key hole and locked with a padlock. This door is strapped inside and out and bolted through the straps about 5" apart, so if woodwork were burned or cut away no one could get through. Circa 1910s, $1-3.

The Sally Port is the only entrance and exit of the Castillo. Directly off the Sally Port are the Spanish guardrooms and the prison. The drawbridge was the primary way of securing the Castillo. By using the cranks located beneath the trapdoors and the counterweights, the drawbridge could be raised and lowered in fifteen minutes by three men. Circa 1910, $1-3.

OLD WATCH TOWER.

The sentry box or watch tower at the corner of the fort provided shelter for men on watch during bad weather. The sentry on duty would give the alarm when an enemy was sighted. Circa 1910s, $1-3.

SA-21—Chapel of St. Mark and Courtyard
Castillo de San Marcos National Monument, St. Augustine, Fla.

This view shows the entrance to the chapel on the left. Circa 1910, $1-3.

The ladies in this 1902 view are playing golf on the grounds surrounding the historic fort. The nine-hole layout of the St. Augustine Golf Club stretched between Riberia Street and the Bay, and included much of the fort green. The course was used by local players and hotel guests from the latter 1800s until well into the twentieth century. This was the first golf course in Florida. Cancelled 1905, $10-12.

Chapter Eleven

Overlooking Matanzas Bay

SEA WALL

This view shows the Monson and Bennett hotels facing the Sea Wall along Bay Street (now Avenida Menendez). The Spanish began construction of the wall but the English completed it in the 1770s. Circa 1920s, $1-3.

Sea Wall, St. Augustine, Fla.

The St. Augustine Sea Wall is four feet wide and one-mile long. It is built of coquina with large slabs of granite on top. The wall provides a promenade along the bay. The Castillo de San Marcos can be seen in the distance. Circa 1910s, $5-7.

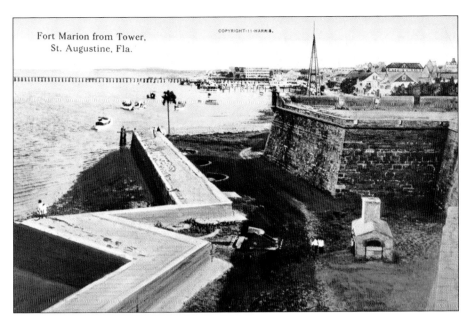

The ancient Spanish fortress, Castillo de San Marcos, overlooks Matanzas Bay and has a commanding control of the Bay entrance from the Atlantic Ocean. Circa 1910s, $1-3.

The 64-foot Victory II tour boat conducted scenic and historical cruises of the St. Augustine waterfront and beautiful Matanzas Bay. Circa 1930s, $1-3.

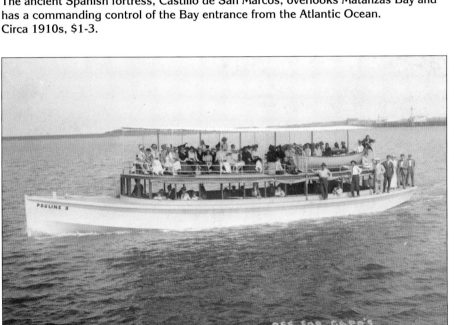

An early 1900s excursion boat giving tourists a view of the St. Augustine waterfront. The Matanzas River, part of the Intercoastal Waterway, separates the central part of St. Augustine with Anastasia Island. Circa 1904, $5-7.

This scene overlooks the Matanzas River near St. Augustine. Cancelled 1913, $1-3.

Chapter Twelve

Getting There: Transportation

Clyde Line Steamer City of Jacksonville, on the St. Johns River, Florida.

Steamboat Sightseers.
In the late 1800s and early 1900s, interest in Florida was high. Florida winters were advertised in newspapers, magazines and books in such glowing terms that areas accessible by steamboat became popular as winter residences for the affluent. With a winter home in Florida, they could escape the snow, ice, and cold of their northern homes. The St. Johns River towns became the most popular winter resorts in the nation. This postcard illustrates the City of Jacksonville steamer bringing visitors to the towns along St. Johns River. Steamboats ran on regular schedules from Jacksonville and many of them stopped at Tocoi, the nearest St. Johns River community to St. Augustine. Circa 1907, $12-14.

On the ST. JOHNS RIVER, Florida.

3114.

Tocoi. From Tocoi, St. Johns River steamboat passengers traveled by rail (St. Johns Railroad) to St. Augustine. This overland trip was made on about eighteen miles of wooden tracks. The train consisted of a car built like a streetcar, a platform car with a canvas top and open sides, and a baggage car, the whole drawn by mules or horses. Circa 1910, $18-20.

Rockledge, Fla. The Plaza Hotel.

Steamboats on the Intercoastal Waterway. During the late 1800s and early 1900s, popular steamboat stopping points between Jacksonville and Palm Beach were St. Augustine, Daytona and Rockledge. This postcard shows the Plaza Hotel, one of the fashionable winter resorts along the East Coast waterway. Cancelled 1908, $8-10.

Florida East Coast Administrative Office. This beautiful building, originally part of the Henry M. Flagler Florida East Coast (FEC) railway system, extended from Jacksonville to Key West. Construction started in 1923 and was completed in December, 1925. Circa 1983, $1-3.

Steamboat Comforts. The bearer of a steamboat ticket was entitled to staterooms, meals, baggage storage, and a fine observation deck. Steamboats gave birth to Florida's tourist industry, only to be left behind by the whims of the Industrial Age and railroad barons like Henry M. Flagler. Cancelled 1925, $5-7.

Florida East Coast Railroad Depot.

Florida East Coast Railway Depot. Horse-drawn carriages are shown lined up beneath the shed covering the passenger platform, waiting for new arrivals at the St. Augustine railroad station. Circa 1903, $5-7.

The "East Coast Champion" of the Florida East Coast Railway is shown behind the E-7 Diesel Electric Unit Number 1019. The Champion, one of many Florida East Coast Name Passenger Trains, served cities on the East Coast of Florida: Jacksonville, St. Augustine, Ormond Beach, Daytona Beach, West Palm Beach and Miami. Circa 1945, $5-7.

Streetcars that ran on rail tracks fronting Flagler's hotels transported visitors to attractions and sites around town. Circa 1907, $13-15.

The First Electric Car ever run in the nation's oldest city. Circa 1907, $18-20.

An Old Landmark of St. Augustine, Florida 25

The Oldest City in the United States

60890

Quaint carriages, dating from the age before automobiles, permitted leisurely rides to points of interest in this ancient city. The drivers were well versed in St. Augustine legend, folk lore and traditions. Circa 1930s, $1-3.

In the 1880s the St. Augustine Transfer Company started offering carriage sightseeing tours to the guests of Henry M. Flagler's hotels. Circa 1930s. $1-3.

209 HOMEWARD BOUND ON THE DIXIE HIGHWAY, FLORIDA.

The Dixie Highway was a network of local and state roads that reached from Michigan to Miami. You could go the whole distance by car in 1915. The Dixie Highway became U.S. Highway 1 in 1927. Circa 1920s, $2-4.

Tin-Can Tourists. A new kind of tourist began visiting Florida in the 1920s. They got their nickname from the tremendous amount of canned beans they ate and the dilapidated mufflers they replaced with discarded tin cans. Cancelled 1924, $5-7.

Early automobile trips to St. Augustine took the adventurous travelers on many moss-draped, tree-lined, roads. Hanging Spanish Moss lent an air of beauty to many of Florida's highways. Circa 1940s, $1-3.

U.S. Highway 1 runs from the Canadian boundary of Maine to southern Florida. It was America's Original Main Street and, in Florida, passed through several East Coast cities including St. Augustine. U.S. Highway 1 was the primary connector of Florida's East Coast from 1929 until about 1970. Circ 1930s, $2-6.

Chapter Thirteen

Where They Worshipped: Churches

Shrine of Nuestra Senora de La Leche. The Shrine was abandoned during border raids by English soldiers stationed in Georgia. It was rebuilt by Bishop Verot in 1873 and blown down by a storm a year later. It was erected by Bishop Curley in 1918. In 1925 Mrs. Hardin restored and furnished it as a chapel in memory of General Martin D. Hardin. Cancelled 1952, $1-3.

The Mission of Nombre de Dios and the Lady of la Leche Shrine are on the site of the landing of Pedro Menendez de Aviles in 1565 where the first Catholic Mass was said. Spanish leader, Pedro Menendez, planted the Cross, Father Fancisco Lopez de Mendoza Grajales offered the first parish Mass, and our American life began. This all took place 55 years before the pilgrims landed at Plymouth Rock. Circa 1945, $1-3.

Shrine of Nuestra Senora de La Leche. By the seventeenth century Timucua Indians were singing Sunday mass in Latin. Circa 1930s, $1-3.

Memorial (Presbyterian) Church, St. Augustine, Fla.

Henry M. Flagler, builder of Florida's East Coast, erected this inspiring example of Venetian Renaissance architecture in 1889 as a memorial to his daughter. Flagler and members of his family lie in the mausoleum of Italian marble. Circa 1930, $1-3.

Memorial Church. The church has one of the finest pipe organs in the country. Circa 1945, $1-3.

FLAGLER MEMORIAL CHURCH
Valencia & Sevilla Sts.
Saint Augustine, Florida

Another view of Memorial Church. Cancelled 1968, $1-3.

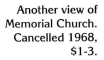

Birds Eye View of St. Augustine, Fla. Looking North from Tower of the Ponce de Leon Hotel

Bird's-Eye View of St. Augustine looking north from the tower of the Ponce de Leon Hotel. The Memorial Church is shown here in the foreground. Circa 1902, $3-5.

CONSTITUTION MONUMENT.   NEW AND OLD SPANISH CATHEDRAL   ST. AUGUSTINE, FLA.
PLAZA.

Your card recived & all members of this church would be delighted sthing to hear from you again I remain — yours truly Mildred Blue. This is the oldest Church in St. Aug. the natives are

Catholic Cathedral and Plaza de La Constitution. This historic structure represents the original Catholic Church dedicated in 1797 becoming a cathedral in 1870. The interior represents the Spanish heritage embellished by ornate décor. Cancelled 1906, $3-5.

CATHEDRAL CHURCH, ST. AUGUSTINE, FLORIDA—6K

Roman Catholic Cathedral. In 1887 the roofs and interior was destroyed by fire but the walls were uninjured. In rebuilding, the north wall was extended and the arms of the cross lengthened. Cancelled 1952, $1-3.

NIGHT SCENE OF CATHOLIC CATHEDRAL. ST. AUGUSTINE, FLORIDA   6

As in all towns of Spanish colonial origin, the stately Cathedral of St. Augustine looks down upon the ancient Plaza de la Constitution. In the Old Moorish façade hang four bells no longer used, the smallest of which bears the inscription: "St. Joseph Ora Pro Nobis A.D. 1682." This is probably the oldest bell in America. Circa 1930, $1-3.

THE OLDEST CITY IN THE UNITED STATES   60871

Another view of the Roman Catholic Cathedral and Plaza. Cancelled 1936, $1-3.

Trinity Episcopal Church. At the corner of St. George and King streets, this was the first Protestant Church to be established in Florida after its acquisition by the United States in 1821. The oldest Episcopal Church in Florida was founded in 1825. Although major remodeling occurred in the early 1900s, the cypress shingle spire remains unchanged and St. Peter's Chapel within commemorates the original parish church and an earlier sanctuary. Circa 1915, $1-3.

Trinity Episcopal Church. This unostentatious bit of English Gothic ecclesiastical architecture stands at the corner of St. George and King streets. The cornerstone was laid in 1825 with portions of the original structure still standing. Cancelled 1949, $1-3.

Another view of Trinity Episcopal Church. Circa 1930s, $1-3.

Casper's Ostrich and Alligator Farm

Casper's Ostrich and Alligator Farm. This attraction, located two miles north of St. Augustine on U.S. Highway 1, contained a large and interesting collection of ostriches, rare birds, alligators, crocodiles and reptiles. Casper's opened as a roadside attraction in 1946. William Casper's Farm was always in the shadow of the established St. Augustine Alligator Farm on nearby Anastasia Island. Casper's never achieved the popularity of its neighbor despite being located on heavily traveled U.S. Highway 1. Circa 1946, $3-5.

Casper's was the only alligator and ostrich farm with an ostrich racetrack. Ostriches were raised and trained at Casper's for racing. Ostrich sulky races were held daily on the .125 mile track. Shown here is William Casper with one of the racers. Circa 1946, $3-5.

THE ROMAN CATHOLIC CATHEDRAL AND PLAZA, ST. AUGUSTINE, FLA.   13657

Another view of the Roman Catholic Cathedral and Plaza.
Cancelled 1936, $1 3.

S.-A. 86 — Trinity Episcopal Church, St. Augustine, Fla.

Trinity Episcopal Church. This unostentatious bit of English Gothic ecclesiastical architecture stands at the corner of St. George and King streets. The cornerstone was laid in 1825 with portions of the original structure still standing. Cancelled 1949, $1-3.

TRINITY EPISCOPAL CHURCH, ST. AUGUSTINE, FLA.

Trinity Episcopal Church. At the corner of St. George and King streets, this was the first Protestant Church to be established in Florida after its acquisition by the United States in 1821. The oldest Episcopal Church in Florida was founded in 1825. Although major remodeling occurred in the early 1900s, the cypress shingle spire remains unchanged and St. Peter's Chapel within commemorates the original parish church and an earlier sanctuary. Circa 1915, $1-3.

Trinity Episcopal Church, St. Augustine, Fla.

The Oldest City in the United States

Another view of Trinity Episcopal Church. Circa 1930s, $1-3.

Casper's Ostrich and Alligator Farm

Casper's Ostrich and Alligator Farm. This attraction, located two miles north of St. Augustine on U.S. Highway 1, contained a large and interesting collection of ostriches, rare birds, alligators, crocodiles and reptiles. Casper's opened as a roadside attraction in 1946. William Casper's Farm was always in the shadow of the established St. Augustine Alligator Farm on nearby Anastasia Island. Casper's never achieved the popularity of its neighbor despite being located on heavily traveled U.S. Highway 1. Circa 1946, $3-5.

Casper's was the only alligator and ostrich farm with an ostrich racetrack. Ostriches were raised and trained at Casper's for racing. Ostrich sulky races were held daily on the .125 mile track. Shown here is William Casper with one of the racers. Circa 1946, $3-5.

SA-5—Casper's Alligator Jungle, St. Augustine, Fla.

A few of the 8,000 alligators at Casper's Ostrich and Alligator Farm. Casper's later changed its name to Casper's Alligator Jungle and in the 1970s simply to the Gatorland Alligator Farm. Circa 1950, $1-3

Alligator Breeders at Casper's Ostrich and Alligator Farm St. Augustine, Fla.

Alligators start breeding usually from the age of 8 to 13 years. These valued specimens are only a few of the many at Casper's. When hungry, these reptiles can be very active and hostile. Otherwise, except during the breeding season, they are about as lazy as a sloth. Circa 1946, $2-4.

"Old Columbus", that Florida Gator

Look Out! Here comes Old Columbus, a large alligator at Casper's in St. Augustine. As shown in this postcard several of the alligator's teeth become quite large with age. Very old alligators, however, lose most of their teeth. An alligator's teeth are not made for chewing, but for catching and holding their prey. Circa 1950, $4-6.

One of the breeding pens at Casper's Ostrich and Alligator Farm. Circa 1950, $1-3.

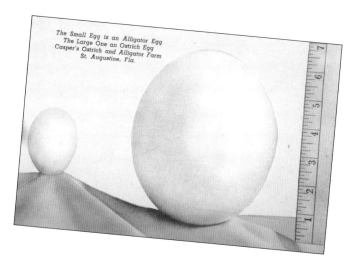

The small egg on the left is an alligator egg, while the large egg on the right is an ostrich egg. Circa 1946, $1-3.

This 8-foot alligator is being put to sleep at Casper's Ostrich and Alligator Farm. Circa 1946, $1-3.

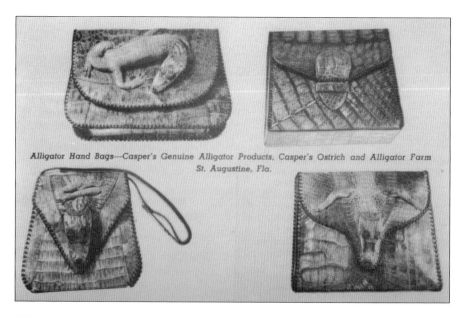

Alligator Hand Bags. The alligator has been used to produce every kind of tourist item imaginable. They have been stuffed and skinned, their hides turned into handbags, fashionable shoes and belts, their claws as purses, their teeth as jewelry and their eggs as curios. This postcard shows some alligator products that were sold at Casper's Ostrich and Alligator Farm. Circa 1950, $1-3.

Six week old ostriches at Casper's Ostrich and Alligator Farm. These mammoth chicks are typical children, calm, quiet one minute, mischievous cut-ups the next. Circa 1946, $2-4.

Ostrich hen and her eggs at Casper's. Circa 1950, $1-3.

Ostriches raised on Casper's Ostrich and Alligator Farm. Ostriches and their cousins, the emus and the rhea, are the largest members of the bird family. Circa 1946, $1-3.

Many rare birds were on display at Casper's. Egyptian ducks, stately swan, African crowned cranes, macaws from Asia, and Florida flamingos were among the Farm's unusual feathered creatures. Circa 1950, $1-3.

Colorful flamingos at Casper's Ostrich and Alligator Farm. Circa 1946, $1-3.

Colorful Flamingos at Casper's Ostrich and Alligator Farm St. Augustine, Fla.

Pelicans at Casper's Ostrich and Alligator Farm St. Augustine, Fla.

Pelicans at Casper's Ostrich and Alligator Farm. Circa 1946, $1-3.

Parrots at Casper's Ostrich and Alligator Fa[rm] St. Augustine, Florida

Parrots at Casper's Ostrich and Alligator Farm. Circa 1946, $1-3

Alligator look-alike, The Crocodile. What is the difference between an alligator and a crocodile? The most striking difference is the shape of the head. The alligator has a broad, rounded snout, while the crocodile snout is narrower and more pointed. Adult alligators are gray-black, while the crocodile is yellowish-gray in color. The crocodile has olive eyes, the alligator eyes are charcoal. Naturalist Dr. William Hornaday near Biscayne Bay in Miami discovered the crocodile in Florida in 1875. Shown here are several crocodiles at Casper's. Circa 1946, $1-3.

CROCODILES -AFRICAN & FLORIDA- MAN EATERS

SA-2—"Man Killers," Crocodiles alive at Casper's Alligator Jungle, St. Augustine, Fla.

Rock Python Snake, 16 Ft. Long, Weight 225 lb.
At Casper's Ostrich and Alligator Farm, St. Augustine

A sixteen foot, 225 pound Rock Python Snake at Casper's Ostrich and Alligator Farm. Circa 1946, $1-3.

Gatorland Alligator Farm. Casper's opened as a roadside attraction in the mid-1940s. This U.S. Highway 1 alligator attraction later became the Gatorland Alligator Farm, which operated until 1982. Circa 1970s, $1-3.

Chapter Fifteen
Early America: Fountain of Youth

The entrance to the Fountain of Youth is located six blocks north of the Castillo de San Marcos. One of the most romantic events in New World History was the search by Juan Ponce de Leon for the Fountain of Youth and his subsequent landing near St. Augustine in 1513. Circa 1930s, $1-3.

The location of the Fountain of Youth has archeological significance, both as the site of the ancient Indian town Seloy and a possible location where Ponce de Leon came ashore and established the Spanish claim to all of North America. Circa 1930s, $1-3.

Indian Burial Ground, Fountain of Youth Park, St. Augustine, Florida 4(

The Oldest City in the United States

Ancient Indian Burial Ground. Protected by a massive reproduction of a Timucua Indian communal house, many Indian burials, excavated by Dr. M. W. Stirling of the Smithsonian Institute, give evidence of the once flowering culture existing before the arrival of Ponce de Leon in 1513. Now covered with soil, for many years over 100 skeletons were exposed in the exact position as they were found. Circa 1930s, $2-4.

Another view of the Fountain of Youth spring well. Circa 1920s, $1-3.

The Fountain of Youth Spring is one of the focal points of the Fountain of Youth, a National Archaeological Park, preserved as a memorial to the Spanish explorer who pioneered the bringing of European civilization to the shores of the United States. Circa 1930s, $1-3.

Another view of the Fountain of Youth spring well. Circa 1930s, $1-3.

The Fountain of Youth spring water was advertised as preserving youth for all that drank the water. Circa 1910s, $1-3.

Spring And Cross. The Fountain of Youth contains foundations and artifacts of the first St. Augustine mission and colony. Located here are the Spring, Cross of Discovery, and the first North American excavated Indian burials. Circa 1930, $1-3.

Scenic Vista. Ancient artifacts and lush vegetation decorate the park-like grounds of the Fountain of Youth. Circa 1945, $1-3.

Preserving Youth.
A humorous postcard of the Fountain of Youth.
Circa 1930s, $2-4.

Chapter Sixteen
Saving History: Museums

The Lightner Museum is housed in the former Alcazar Hotel built in 1888 by Henry M. Flagler as a companion to the Ponce de Leon across the street. Closed as a hotel in 1930, the building was purchased in 1947 by Otto C. Lightner who donated it and his fabulous collections to the citizens of St. Augustine. Mr. Lightner died in 1950 and is buried in the courtyard. Circa 1930s, $2-4.

Lightner Museum. Enter the glittering era of St. Augustine in the "Gay 90s." Circa 1930s, $2-4.

The Vedder House was acquired by the St. Augustine Historical Society in 1899 and made into a museum. The Nicholas Vedder collection of ancient maps and relics were on display. The building, which bordered on Treasury Street, burned down in 1914. Circa 1910s, $6-8.

Lightner Museum. The museum's unique offerings include natural history, fine arts, ceramics, glass, furniture, toys, musical instruments and thousands of other unusual objects. Circa 1940s, $1-3.

Ripley's Believe It or Not! The Ripley Museum contains a large collection of oddities and curiosities assembled from many parts of the world by Robert L. Ripley. Circa 1930s, $3-5.

A more modern view of Ripley's Believe It Or Not Museum. Circa 1950s, $1-3.

Within the walls of the Zorayda Castle are fabulous treasures from all over the world and sights like the forbidden Harem Quarters. Circa 1940s, $2-4.

Zorayda Castle, St. Augustine, Florida

Zorayda Castle. Enchanted palace of the Moors. Architect Franklin Smith designed the building to reproduce a portion of the famed Alhambra in Spain. It is now a museum that contains rare oriental art treasures collected by the late A.S. Mussallem. Circa 1940s, $2-4.

The Oldest Store Museum, in its 1800s surroundings, has more than 100,000 items of general store merchandise on display. It is a re-creation of a late-19th century general store. Circa 1940s, $2-4.

Education: Flagler College

Flagler College. Two years after St. Augustine's 400th birthday, the magnificent, stately Ponce de Leon Hotel closed its doors. Motels had taken the place of grand hotels and tourist attractions farther south competed with St. Augustine. The building, however, was in good shape. Henry M. Flagler had spent an unnecessary amount of money in constructing the hotel with the hope that it would withstand the test of time. Over 100 years after its construction, the building stands largely unaffected by time. Flagler's reflection proved to be correct. In 1968, the hotel and numerous structures surrounding the main building became Flagler College. The college opened as a private four-year liberal arts college for girls. Circa 1960s, $2-4.

Entrance To Flagler College. The college invested more than $30 million in the development and restoration of its unique campus. Private donations for restoration were also contributed by the Kenan Foundation, established by the family of Flagler's third wife, Mary Lily Kenan. Students and faculty congregate for meals in the grand dining room amidst antique furnishings from the hotel as light filters through the famous Louis Tiffany stained glass windows. Circa 1960s, $2-4.

The first electric hotel clock in the nation is still in operation in the elegant parlor where Flagler once entertained privately and where today's students and their parents often meet. Circa 1980s, $1-3.

Henry Flagler Statue. This statue, which now stands by the entrance to Flagler College, was erected by the National Railroad Historical Society on February 23, 1959. Copyright 1983, $1-3.

Another view of Flagler college. Circa 1980s, $1-3.

Chapter Eighteen

Florida's Favorite Fruit: Citrus

7884. ORANGES AND BLOSSOMS

To Libbie from C. a. Dodge

DR. GARNETT'S ORANGE GROVE, ST. AUGUSTINE, FLA.

This famous orange grove, just north of the City Gate, was planted by Dr. Ruben B. Garnett shortly after his arrival in St. Augustine around 1883. The orange grove was a major tourist attraction. Cancelled 1914, $3-5.

Florida is one of the few places in the world where citrus can be grown. The early Spaniards brought oranges to Florida and planted them near St. Augustine. By the early 1800s citrus growers had begun to ship the fruit commercially. By 1886 production for the first time had reached an annual production of a million boxes. Within the span of a few years, Florida increased the volume and was able to produce several million boxes of tree-ripened fruit and ship them to markets in northern cities within the same week in which they were harvested. Today, the citrus industry is second only to tourism as Florida's most important industry and is one of the backbones of Florida's economy. Circa 1903, $1-3.

GARNETT ORANGE GROVE DRIVE, ST. AUGUSTINE, FLA.
COPYRIGHT 1906 BY W. J. HARRIS.

Under the Spanish moss-covered oaks to the Garnett Orange Grove was one of the most beautiful and interesting drives in the city. Copyright 1906, $1-3.

Picking Oranges at Garnetts Orange Grove. St. Augustine, Fla.

The Oldest City in the United States   .62

The Garnett Orange Grove in the heart of the city was one of the show places of St. Augustine. Tourists could pick their own oranges from the trees. Cancelled 1941, $1-3.

9092 PICKING ORANGES.

The sender of this card, mailed in St. Augustine in 1912, said "Mr. Sylvester sent you a box of oranges because he thought you would all enjoy them." Shown here are migrant workers picking fruit. After the fruit is picked, the workers often leave Florida. They work their way North, picking crops as they go. Migrant workers and their families have a hard life, since wages are low and they often cannot find work. Cancelled 1912, $1-3.

Passing through Orange Grove, Florida.

A steam powered train passing through an orange grove. Railroads made it possible for citrus groves to be planted in the interior away from rivers. This expanded the acres planted. Markets began to open up in northern cities for oranges and other citrus fruits and Florida soon became the major exporter of citrus fruit.
Cancelled 1928, $10-12.

In the early 1900s, tourists visiting Florida often sent home a crate of oranges or at least a postcard showing a crate of oranges. And so it is that the original orange tree, which once was grown only to grace the imperial regal gardens of ancient Oriental rulers, has become today one of the most valuable and widely grown fruits of international commerce. Cancelled 1912, $3-5.

The Box of Oranges I promised to send you from Florida.

FLORIDA ORANGES

GREETINGS FROM FLORIDA

Chapter Nineteen

Leisure Time: Entertainment and Recreation

In 1922 the Villa Zorayda, a house built by Franklin W. Smith, became a nightclub and gambling casino. The Zorayda Club closed in 1925 when Florida outlawed gambling. In 1936, it was opened as a tourist attraction called the Zorayda Castle. Circa 1920s, $5-7.

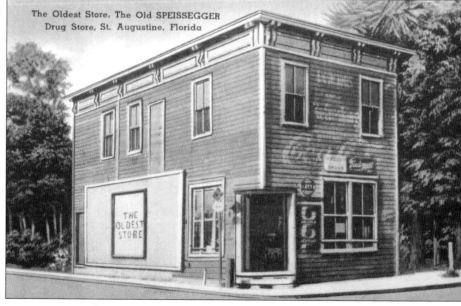

The old Speissegger Drug Store, located at 31 Orange Street near the City Gate, is a cypress-sided building erected about 1886. Mechanical figures guide visitors through the early years of St. Augustine medicine. Circa 1940s, $1-3.

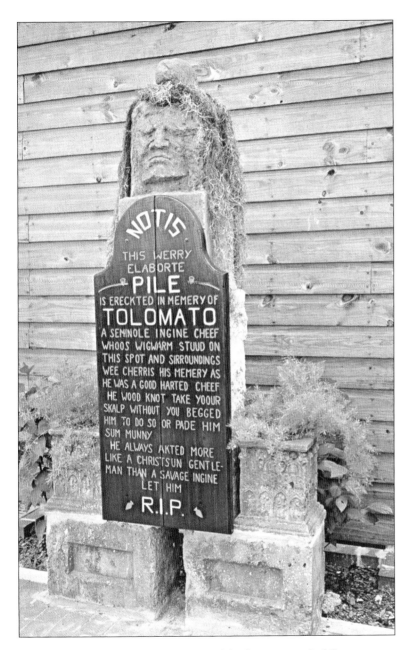

The Old Jail, completed in 1891 and built with funds provided by railroad magnate Henry M. Flagler, housed prisoners for over sixty years. One of the surviving nineteenth century jails. Here, the early sheriff, Joe Perry, and his wife Lou, lived and worked for $2 a day. The Old Jail was placed on the National Registry of Historic Places in 1987. Circa 1930s, $3-5.

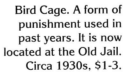

Bird Cage. A form of punishment used in past years. It is now located at the Old Jail. Circa 1930s, $1-3.

Tolomato. This monument was created in the courtyard of the Oldest Drug Store April 1, 1893 by T. W. Speissegger. South of this monument is the cemetery started in 1784, and known as Tolomato Cemetery. Circa 1940s, $1-3.

Prisoner Workshop in the Old Jail. This postcard view shows the original workshop where prisoners made their own shackles and rough caskets. Circa 1940s, $1-3.

Old Chain Gang Wagon. The wagon was actually used to lock prisoners in while on road detail. It is on display at the Old Jail. Circa 1940s, $2-4.

Chapter Twenty

St. Augustine Seashore: Anastasia Island

Station for Anastasia, South, Chautauqua and Crescent Beaches

The wooden bridge to Anastasia Island was a welcome convenience when constructed in 1895. Pedestrians and bicyclists crossed for only five cents; toll for a double team and driver began at twenty-five cents, with an additional five-cent charge per person. The St. Johns Electric Company later laid tracks across the bridge, carrying passengers five miles down the island to South St. Augustine Beach. Electric streetcars transported passengers around the St. Augustine area from 1906 to the 1920s. In 1927 this bridge was replaced with the Bridge of Lions, which added a touch of old world charm to the Bay front as it linked Anastasia Island to the ancient city. Circa 1910s, $10-12

OLD HORSE CAR—USINA'S NORTH BEACH, ST. AUGUSTINE, FLA.   3345-29

This Horse-drawn Railroad Car was located at Usina's North Beach on Anastasia Island near St. Augustine. The boat landing was reached by a five mile boat ride from St. Augustine. This quaint old car took visitors from the boat landing to the ocean beach, a distance of about a third of a mile. No charge was made for its use and the proceeds from the sale of this postcard were used for its upkeep. Note the horse pulling the train from the side and not from the front. Circa 1915, $10-12.

One of the city's most familiar landmarks, the St. Augustine Lighthouse was one of a series of lighthouses constructed along the Atlantic coastline during the mid-nineteenth century. The first order lighthouse, 165 feet high, marks the entrance to the port of St. Augustine and guides coastal vessels on their course. Circa 1920s, $1-3.

ANASTASIA LIGHTHOUSE, NEAR ST. AUGUSTINE

Old Spanish Fort Ruins. At Matanzas Inlet, eighteen miles south of St. Augustine, lies the ruins of an Old Spanish Fort that defended the sea approach to St. Augustine from the south. Cancelled 1908, $10-12.

St. Augustine's Inlet to the sea was treacherous. Its shifting sands, called "crazy banks," were the dread of all who sailed to the ancient city. The St. Augustine Lighthouse, with its black and white spirals was built in 1874 and replaced the original coquina tower which was destroyed by the sea. For more than a century now, this spiral-striped tower has been an unforgettable landmark for visitors by land and sea. The light remains active and is visible from twenty miles away. Circa 1945. $1-3.

Fort Matanzas. Once decayed and crumbling, this old landmark bears mute testimony of that historic period when the Spaniards were heroically struggling to defend St. Augustine against the invader. Militant English colonists were a constant menace and it was primarily to repel a possible attack from that "back door" quarter that Fort Matanzas was erected between the years 1740-1742. Just inside Matanzas Inlet, on Rattlesnake Island, it is eighteen miles south of the Castillo de San Marcos and St. Augustine. Fort Matanzas guarded the "back door" to St. Augustine. Today it is a national monument. Circa 1940s, $1-3.

St. Augustine Alligator Farm

Whitney's Ponce de Leon Spring, St. Augustine, Fla.

In the 1890s a museum of marine curiosities was located on Anastasia Island. Part of this museum was Everett C. Whitney's "Burning Spring." Whitney's attraction was simply an artesian well pouring forth highly sulfuric water. Mixed with gasoline and ignited, the stream issued a blue flame, a phenomenon that seemed unexplainable to the visitors who observed it. The burning spring remained a fixture at the attraction for years. Whitney later opened an Alligator Farm next to the museum. Whitney along with George Reddington and Felix Fire turned the attraction into the St. Augustine Alligator Farm. Circa early 1900s, $18-20.

St. Augustine Alligator Farm. This St. Augustine attraction is listed on the National Register of Historic Places. It has the world's largest collection of alligators and crocodiles. At this attraction on Anastasia Island, two miles south of the Bridge of Lions, visitors can explore the habitat of alligators, crocodiles, giant tortoises, birds, and snakes. The farm, established in 1893, has always been one of Florida's favorite attractions. The "Mission" style main building of the St. Augustine Alligator Farm, pictured here, has been a landmark along U.S. Highway A1A for more than seventy years. It was built in 1937. Circa 1945, $1-3.

A True Piece of Floridiana. For over a century, visitors to the St. Augustine Alligator Farm have thrilled to the sight of its ferocious looking alligators. They generally become aroused only in the presence of food or physical threat and otherwise prefer to laze in the water or lay about near it. Circa 1940s, $2-4.

Just a few of the alligators found at the St. Augustine Alligator Farm. The farm contains about 6,000 alligators ranging from babies to gators fourteen feet long. Circa 1940s, $1-3.

Known around the World. Thousands of servicemen who visited the Alligator Farm during World War II helped to broadcast its popularity. Circa 1940s, $1-3.

An alligator is about to get its teeth brushed, as an alligator handler and alligator perform for visitors at the St. Augustine Alligator Farm. Circa 1920s, $10-12.

No Trespassing on this island at the St. Augustine Alligator Farm. Circa 1940s, $1-3.

BIRD ROOKERY

Greetings from
St. Augustine Alligator Farm

This postcard of Chris Lightburn with an alligator shows two popular publicity shots at the Alligator Farm. Lightburn was for many years a skilled alligator handler at the attraction. Circa 1960s, $2-4.

Alligators are not the only reason people visit the St. Augustine Alligator Farm. Birds are an important part of this landmark attraction. The Farm's two-acre real-Florida swamp habitat is the breeding ground for several water birds to nest and raise their young every spring. The wild bird rookery is in full breeding plumage from mid-March to July. Herons, egrets, ibis, roseate spoonbills, and wood storks find comfort in building their nests in the trees, with alligators below, providing protection from the natural predators such as opossums, snakes, and raccoons. Circa 1940s, $1-3.

The Giant Galapagos Tortoise, now almost extinct because of slaughtering by pirates, whalers and fishermen, is a survivor of the prehistoric age. The St. Augustine Alligator Farm maintains one of the world's largest groups of living Galapagos tortoises. Here, under scientifically controlled conditions, the breeding of this species is being carried on successfully. These tortoises weigh up to 500 pounds, are vegetarian and have a life span of several centuries. Circa 1930s, $2-4.

Florida Pets, Alligators taking a Sun Bath.

The alligator is probably the most picturesque and popular feature of the Florida peninsula. Alligators are truly wild and dangerous animals that deserve the respect of humans. They have big teeth, and their jaw muscles are so powerful that the strongest person on earth cannot pull them apart. Their jaws can slam shut with as much pressure as 2,000 pounds per square inch. Cancelled 1943, $1-3.

Chapter Twenty-Two

Aquatic Attraction: Marineland

Marine Studios, more commonly known as Marineland and located 18 miles south of St. Augustine, is Florida's famous Oceanarium where thousands of marine specimens live together as they do in the open sea. Visitors may walk about on top of the Oceanarium or study the ever changing panorama of deep sea life through more than 200 portholes at varying levels. Circa 1940s, $3-5.

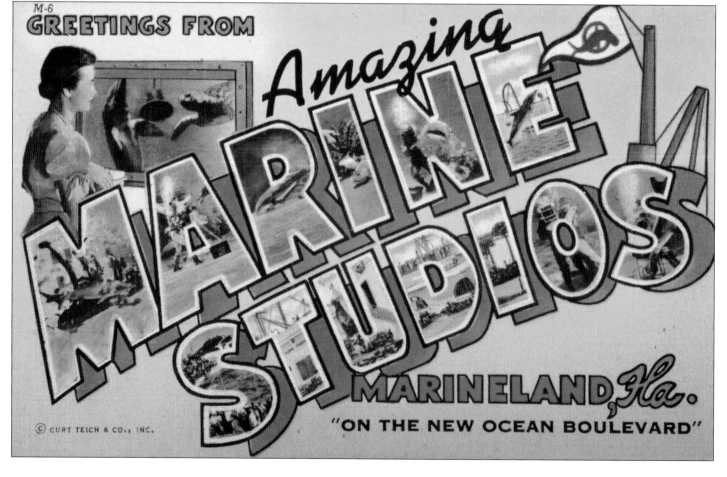

An aerial view of Marineland, the world's first Oceanarium, which is located on U.S. Highway A1A between the Atlantic Ocean and Florida's Inland Waterway (Matanzas River). Fish live in two huge tanks connected by a flume. The tanks are maintained to approximate conditions of marine life in the open sea. Circa 1940s, $3-5.

High jumping bottle-nose dolphins, or porpoises, as they are commonly called are known and beloved by mariners. These friendly air-breathing, warm-blooded mammals were first introduced into prolonged captivity at Marineland. Marineland, which opened in 1938, was added to the National Historic Register in 1986. Circa 1945, $1-3.

M-17—Through the Hoop with "Flippy" at Marine Studios, Marineland, Florida

Flippy, the educated porpoise, performed amazing stunts six days a week, at Marineland. Flippy was caught south of Daytona Beach in a section of the Intercoastal Waterway, a favorite feeding ground of inshore porpoises, which ride the flooding and ebbing tides to prey on schools of fish. At 7-feet, 270-pounds, Flippy grew to 8-feet and added 120 pounds in captivity. Circa 1940s, $3-5.

MOUTH TO MOUTH FEEDING AT MARINE STUDIOS, MARINELAND, FLA.

A Shark arrives at Marine Studios, Marineland, Fla. — K-69-D-1

A Shark arrives at Marineland. A fishing fleet, owned and operated by Marineland, was in constant search of new specimen for observation. After a shark was captured it was transported to the Oceanarium, as shown in this postcard view, and released into the receiving tank. After a preliminary examination, it was turned loose in the Oceanarium. Circa 1940s, $1-3.

Mouth To Mouth Feeding. Showing the faith that the regular feeders have in the famed jumping porpoises, a Marineland attendant leans far over the water with the tail of a blue-runner in his mouth, as a porpoise gently accepts the fish. Circa 1940s, $2-4.

M-8—Mother and Baby Porpoise at Marine Studios, Marineland, Florida

Mother and baby porpoise are inseparable companions in this ever-changing exhibit of marine life at Marineland. The first successful birth in captivity took place at Marineland in 1947. Circa 1940s, $2-4.

M-9—A Scene in the 7-Ton Coral Reef at Marine Studios, Marineland, Florida

Here are shown a grouper and a queen angle fish seeking safety in the reproduced 7-ton coral reef at Marineland. Circa 1940s, $1-3.

M-2—"Pudgy," the Porpoise, at Marine Studios, Marineland, Fla.

Pudgy, the porpoise, leaps high with glee at his home in the giant Oceanarium at Marineland. Porpoises are natural clowns, the jokesters of the deep. They love to tease other specimens in the Oceanarium. Circa 1940s, $1-3.

SHARKS AND SHIPWRECKS AT MARINE STUDIOS, MARINELAND, FLORIDA F 127

Porpoises, rays, giant sharks, turtles, reef and tropical fish parade in bright review. In one end of the huge rectangular Oceanarium over 7-tons of coral, sea fans, and plumes duplicate a coral reef. In the center of the large tank, resting forlornly on the sand-covered bottom, lie the remains of a sunken ship, its barnacled ribs and bowspirit offering shelter for sheepshead, jewfish and drum.
Cancelled 1951, $1-3.

M-3 Diver and Shark at Marine Studios, Marineland, Fla.

Giant sharks are hypodermically drugged upon capture for Marineland. Here is shown a diver walking a drugged shark to revive it from the effects of the drug. In the foreground a giant grouper takes his afternoon siesta. Circa 1940s, $3-5.

Top Deck Crowd at Marine Studios

A crowd watches the porpoise jump from the water to snatch food from the attendant's hand. Circa 1940s. $3-5.

Chapter Twenty-Three

More Faces of St. Augustine

ST. AUGUSTINE, Fla. Plaza and Market.

From the early 1600s St. Augustine's Plaza has functioned as a community area for meetings and recreation.
Circa 1910, $5-7.

SA-25—Old City Gates, St. Augustine, Fla.

An 1880 view of the old city gate. Circa 1945, $1-3.

1880 The City Gate St. Augustine, Florida

Old City Gate. During the days of Spanish occupation St. Augustine's inner line of defense consisted of a wall extending from the Castillo de San Marcos to the San Sebastian River. As the town was surrounded on three sides by water, the gate offered, at that time, the only entrance to the city. Circa 1930s, $1-3.

Old City Gate. Now a part of the Castillo de San Marcos National Monument, these pillars are the only remnants of an earthwork first built in the early 1700s. Circa 1930s, $1-3.

At the Old City Gates, St. Augustine, Florida

48

The Oldest City in the United States
Copyright P. A. Wolfe, 1939

Celebration of Ponce de Leon.
Founding of the City, St. Augustine, Fla.

An annual Ponce de Leon celebration was held along the downtown waterfront and drew large crowds. These celebrations began in the 1880s and continued until the early 1930s. Circa 1910, $7-9.

SA.66—Old Slave Market
St. Augustine, Fla.
Oldest City in the United States

A public market was established in the Plaza de la Constitution by the Spanish Governor de Canzo in 1598, together with a standard system of weights and measures, operating here until late in the nineteenth century. Minutes of the City Council 1821-1861 show that a few slaves were bought and sold there. In the early days ships unloaded nearby and their cargoes were offered alongside produce from the countryside. The present structure is a replica of one burned in 1887. Circa 1930s, $1-3.

SA-33—Ancient Catholic Cemetery of Tolomato
St. Augustine, Fla.

Tolomato Indian Village. A map of the city of St. Augustine dated May 15, 1737, describes the site of Tolomato Cemetery as the "church and village of Tolomato, an Indian village served by the Franciscan Priests." The church was built of wood, but had a four-story coquina stone Bell Tower. When Florida was turned over to the British in 1763, the Spaniards and the Indians left, together with their Priests. Tolomato Church was torn down by the British troops for firewood, but the Tower survived until the 1790s when, it is traditionally believed, the stones were used in the construction of the present Cathedral. The Christian Tolomato Indians had buried their dead near the church and village. Circa 1930s, $1-3.

DADE MONUMENT
MILITARY CEMETERY AT THE BARRACKS
ST. AUGUSTINE, FLA.

ANCIENT SPANISH SHRINE OF
NUESTRA SENORA DE LA LECHE,
ST. AUGUSTINE, FLORIDA—66

Mission Cemetery. A small cemetery is located near the Shrine of Nuestra Senora de La Leche. Six Federal soldiers were interred during and after the Civil War (1861-1865). Burials here were only occasional until the closing years of the 19th Century, and most graves are those of Parishioners who died between the years 1880-1900. Circa 1930s, $1-3.

Military Cemetery. The dead from Major Dade's detachment during the Second Seminole War (1835-1842) were buried on the battlefield, but seven years later, their remains were relocated to the National Cemetery in St. Augustine where a memorial now stands. The National Cemetery is Florida's oldest national military burial ground. Circa 1910, $5-7.

Slaves Freed. During the Civil War, St. Augustine fell into Union hands in March of 1862. In January of 1863, President Abraham Lincoln's Emancipation Proclamation was officially issued in Florida at a location within the boundary of the present day Old St. Augustine Village. This action freed all slaves in Florida. Circa 1910s, $5-7.

Y.M.C.A. Circa 1910s, $3-5.

The back of the card reads, "New Flagler Hospital. Completed in 1920. One of the finest and best equipped in the country." Circa 1920s, $3-5.

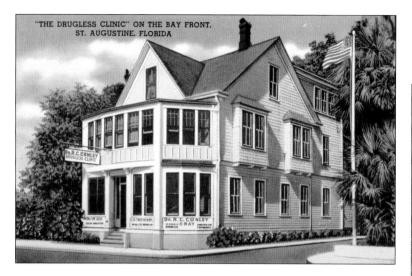

The Drugless Clinic. The clinic was operated by Dr. R. C. Conley, at 12 Bay Street, almost directly opposite the Castillo de San Marcos. The Clinic was equipped to diagnose and treat 98 percent of all human ailments, and was one of the finest and most modern in the south. The Clinic specialized in the diagnosis and treatment of difficult cases. Cancelled 1942, $3-5.

711 - Happy Hours at the Seashore.

St. Augustine Beach is located across the Bridge of Lions from the nation's oldest city. Here miles of white sand ocean beach are to be found. During the early 1900s automobiles could be driven and parked on the hard packed sand. Beach attire has changed over the years, but so has the concept of "bathing." The above St. Augustine scene depicts the popularity of the beach for swimmers, surfers and ocean play in the early 20th century. Circa 1910, $3-5.

Winter Surf Bathing in Florida.

3190.

Beaches were one of the reasons people came to Florida in the early 1900s and these bathers seem to be enjoying the beach in St. Augustine. Circa 1905, $5-7.

The St. Augustine Beach is about fifteen miles long and, in places, over 500 feet wide. Circa 1940s, $1-3.

Greetings From St. Augustine Beach. Shown in this beach view is the Fishing Pier. Circa 1945, $1-3.

Dinner Time for the Sea Gulls. Circa 1930s, $1-3.

Florida Tourists.

Photo copyright 1907. The Hugh C. Leighton Co.

Sea Oats and Sand. Beautiful white, sandy beach at St. Augustine Beach. Circa 1945, $1-3.

White Tiger and His Alligators. This card was mailed in St. Augustine in 1905. The alligator has been called the most valuable wild animal in Florida. Cancelled 1905, $3-5.

Alligators were a popular subject from the viewpoint of Florida postcard publishers. In the early 1900s, when picture postcards were at the height of their popularity, millions went through the postal system daily. Both photographers and artist-drawn alligator scenes went on sale for locals and tourists to buy and send. Well-known comic artists used alligator situations as the basis of postcard cartoons. Cancelled 1910, $20-25.

A Note About Postcards

Postcards had their beginning in Austria in 1869. The United States government began to issue postcards in 1873. The cards were stamped on one side to provide for the address and left blank on the other side. The picture postcard did not come into common use in the United States until after 1900. It was about 1902 that the postcard craze hit the country; it lasted until the U. S. entered World War I in the spring of 1917. Collectors would send postcards to total strangers in faraway places, asking local cards in return. Some collectors specialized in railroad depots, street scenes, cemeteries, churches, courthouses, farms, amusement parks, rivers, steamboats, plants, agricultural products, even comic cards; others collected anything they could find. Postcard albums, bought by the millions, were filled with every sort of postcard ever issued. The craze was actually worldwide, since many countries had postcards.

Before March 1, 1907, it was illegal to write any message on the same side of the card as the address. For that reason the early postcards often have handwriting all over the sides of the picture and sometimes right across it. Many beautiful cards were defaced in this way. When postcards first started to go through the mail, they were postmarked at the receiving post office as well as that of the sender, making it easy to see the time involved between post offices—sometimes remarkably brief! The volume of postcards was an important reason for discontinuing the unnecessary second marking about 1910. For years postcards cost only a nickel for six and the postage was a penny, right up to World War II.

The most popular American postcards up to World War I were those made in Germany from photographs supplied by American publishers. At the time of the postcard craze, of course, color photography was still something of a rarity and not commercially viable. For the color cards, black and white photos were touched up, hand-colored, and then generally reproduced by lithography. Lithography consists of transferring the image to a lithographic stone, offset to a rubber blanket, and then printed onto paper. The details in the German produced cards were extremely sharp, and the best of them technically have never been matched since.

The German postcard industry folded in the summer of 1914, when the war struck Europe, and never revived. Three years later, the United States entered the war, and the postcard craze ended.

Postcards printed in America were generally of a poorer quality and had a white border. These white border cards were produced until about 1930 when the "linen" textured card was introduced. While this card was less expensive to produce, it also reduced the clarity of detail in the pictures. After 1945 the "chrome" card with a glossy finish replaced the linen card. This type of finish allowed for a very sharp reproduction of the picture. In 1970, a king-sized chrome card (4-inch by 5.875-inch) was introduced and by 1978 it was in general use everywhere.

Bibliography

Adams, William R. and Paul L. Weaver, III. *Historical Places of St. Augustine and St. Johns County*. St. Augustine, Florida: Southern Heritage Press, 1993.

Arana, Luis Rafael and Albert Macucy. *The Building of Castillo de San Marcos*. St. Augustine: Eastern National Park & Monument Association, 1977.

Arnade, Charles W. *The Siege of St. Augustine in 1702*. Gainesville, Florida: University of Florida Press, 1959.

Ayers, R. Wayne. *Florida's Grand Hotels from the Guilded Age*. Charleston, South Carolina: Arcadia Publishing, 2005.

Bierstadt, Edward. *Picturesque St. Augustine*. New York, New York: Artotype Publishing Company, 1891.

Bryant, William C. *St. Augustine: A Guided Tour of America's Oldest City*. Picturesque America, 1872.

Chorlian, Meg, Editor. *St. Augustine: America's Oldest City*. Peterborough, New Hampshire: Cobblestone Publishing, Inc., 1995.

Colee, Schelia. *Historic Churches in St. Augustine*. St. Augustine: Self-published, 1984.

Dewhurst, William W. *The History of St. Augustine Florida*. New York: G. P. Putnam's Sons, 1885.

Fretwell, Jacquelin K., Editor. *Civil War Times in St. Augustine*. Port Salerno, Florida: Florida Classics Library, 1988.

Graham, Thomas. *St. Augustine, 1867*. St. Augustine: St. Augustine Historical Society, 1996.

Green, Paul. *Cross and Sword, 1565-1965*. St. Augustine, Florida: St. Augustine's 400th Anniversary, Inc., 1965.

Hall, Maggi Smith. *Flavors of St. Augustine*. Lake Buena Vista: Tailored Tours Publications, Inc., 1999.

Hall, Maggi Smith and the St. Augustine Historical Society. *St. Augustine*. Charleston, South Carolina: Arcadia Publishing, 2002.

Harvey, Karen. *St. Augustine and St. Johns County*. Virginia Beach, Virginia: Donning Company, Publishers, 1980.

Helfrick, Robb. *St. Augustine Impressions*. Helena, Montana: Farcountry Press, 2004.

Historic Catholic Sites of St. Augustine. St. Augustine: Parish of the Cathedral of St. Augustine, 1988.

Laffal, Ken. *St. Augustine On My Mind*. Helena, Montana: Falcon Publishing Company, 2001.

Lee, W. Howard. *The Story of Old St. Augustine*. St. Augustine: Record Press, Inc., 1951.

Puckett, Ron, Rod Morris and Mary Lou Phillips. *Yesterday in St. Augustine*. Tallahassee, Florida: Yesterday in Florida, Inc., 2003.

Reynolds, Charles B. *The Standard Guide: St. Augustine*. St. Augustine: Historic Print & Map Company, 2004.

Seeing St. Augustine. New York, New York: AMS Press Inc., 1937.

Spencer, Donald D. *St. Augustine: A Picture Postcard History*. Ormond Beach: Camelot Publishing, 2002.

Steen, Sandra and Susan Steen. *Historic St. Augustine*. Parsippany, New Jersey: Dillon Press, 1997.

Stewart, Laura and Susanne Hupp. *Florida Historic Homes*. Orlando, Florida: Sentinel Communications Company, 1988.

Van Campen, J. T. *St. Augustine: Florida's Colonial Capital*. St. Augustine: St. Augustine Historical Society, 1959.

Voelbricht, John L. *St. Augustine's Historical Heritage As Seen Today*. St. Augustine: C. F. Hamblen, Inc., 1952.

Waterbury, Jean Parker, Editor. *The Oldest City*. St. Augustine: St. Augustine Historical Society, 1983.

Waterbury, Jean Parker. *The Oldest House*. St. Augustine: St. Augustine Historical Society, 1984.

Wiles, Jon W. *Invisible Saint Augustine*. St. Augustine, Florida: Self-published, 1992.

Wyllie, H. S. St. *Augustine Under Three Flags*. St. Augustine, Florida: Self-published, 1898.

Index